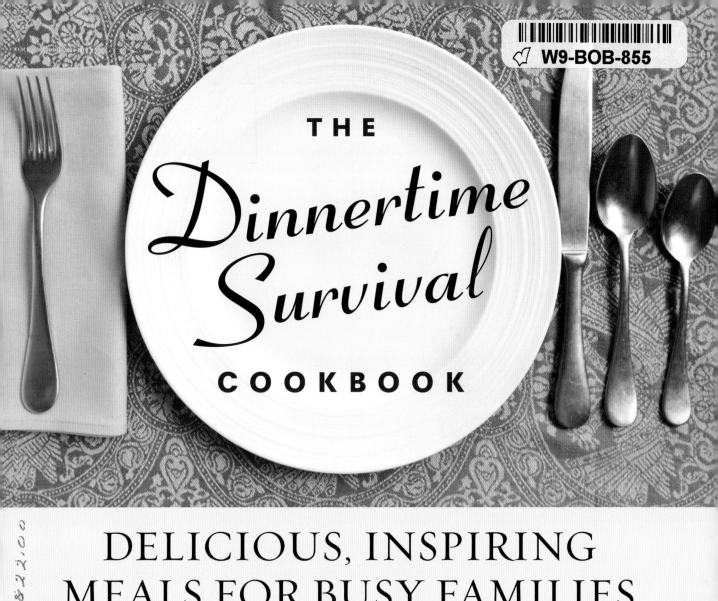

THE
Dinnertime Survival
COOKBOOK

DELICIOUS, INSPIRING MEALS FOR BUSY FAMILIES

Debra Ponzek with Mary Goodbody

Running Press
PHILADELPHIA · LONDON

Published by Running Press,
A Member of the Perseus Books Group

Books published by Running Press are available at special
discounts for bulk purchases in the United States by corp-
orations, institutions, and other organizations. For more
information, please contact the Special Markets Department
at the Perseus Books Group, 2300 Chestnut Street, Suite 200,
Philadelphia, PA 19103, or call (800) 810-4145, ext. 5000,
or e-mail special.markets@perseusbooks.com.

ISBN 978-0-7624-4475-5
Library of Congress Control Number: 2012942522
E-book ISBN 978-0-7624-4827-2

9 8 7 6 5 4 3 2 1
Digit on the right indicates the number of this printing

Cover and interior design by Corinda Cook
Edited by Kristen Green Wiewora

Photography by Steve Legato
Food Styling by Deborah Wahl
     Assistant Food Stylist: Karen Wilson Lynch
Prop Styling by Mariellen Melker
     Prop Styling Assistant: Marcy Miksic

The publisher would like to extend special thanks to Anthony
and John and also to Crate and Barrel, King of Prussia, PA,
and Nannygoat Antiques, Narberth, PA.

Typography: Requiem, Maxima, Ribbon, and Shaker

Running Press Book Publishers
2300 Chestnut Street
Philadelphia, PA 19103-4371

Visit us on the web!
www.runningpresscooks.com

To my sister, Gail,
whose sense of humor,
love, and friendship
I treasure every day.

CONTENTS

ACKNOWLEDGMENTS

THANKS TO:

Mary Goodbody, who knows how to make magic out of my thoughts and words. Your beautiful writing and fun spirit make it enjoyable to work together.

My agent, Jane Dystel, who has been a longtime supporter. She always knows how to point me in the right direction.

Kristen Green Wiewora, my editor, whose enthusiasm for the book saw me through the process of writing it.

Sarabeth Levine, whose creative spirit and exceptional knowledge of baking were so helpful to me during recipe testing.

Cyril Chaminade, our talented pastry chef, and the pastry team at Aux Délices for help testing and retesting recipes and for coming up with such great ideas.

The chefs and staff at Aux Délices, who were so helpful during the process of writing the book and who understood that my time constraints were even crazier than usual.

Lynn Manheim, who shared many of the excellent recipes from her collection with me.

My wonderful husband, Greg, who is always willing to try a recipe "one more time." Best of all, his love and passion for food match my own.

My children Remy, Cole, and Gray, who thankfully feel free to offer their culinary opinions and who were such good sports while I tested (and asked them to sample) recipes. I will always love cooking for you.

Finally, my parents, Phil and Marion Ponzek, who understood and joined in my enthusiasm for food, even from an early age. I will always be grateful.

INTRODUCTION

I started my professional life as a restaurant chef, moved on to entrepreneur and caterer—and along the way became a wife and mother. I guess you could say I have been around the culinary block. Like most of you, I wear many hats. My husband, Greg Addonizio, and I own a business in Connecticut called Aux Délices, which has four stores where we offer company-branded, prepared foods and a hand-picked collection of specialty foods. We also cater and give cooking classes for both adults and kids. All this keeps us extremely busy.

On the home front, I feed a hungry and growing family . . . nearly every day of every week of the year. I may be a highly trained chef but nonetheless, there are times when it is a struggle to come up with ideas for what to cook for dinner. I may be crazy-busy but because I believe in cooking—and, frankly, love to cook—I came up with this collection of easy recipes that, I hope, appeal to most home cooks. Many are quick, but not all. My cooking is more about flavor, balance, and appeal than time-saving strategies, although I also pass these along as they pertain to my recipes. As I am sure is true of many of my readers, there are times when I realize I am cooking the same-old same-old, week after week. When that particular lightbulb goes off in my brain, I purposely come up with something out of the ordinary, very often using ingredients and flavor combinations I know and love. A lot of these dishes found their way into *The Dinnertime Survival Cookbook*.

How do we get "stuck" with the five or six recipes we know how to cook? Easy. We usually have the ingredients needed for our standard chicken dish, meatloaf, or spaghetti with meatballs and so that's what we make. I recently read that more than half of us make the same dish at least once a week, and more often than not, we cook chicken!

Aren't there times when you yearn to change it up? Sure, we all love our time-tested recipes using pasta and ground beef, but who wants to make the same thing week in and week out? That's what this book is all about: easy, accessible recipes that you can add to your weekly rotation. That will help you survive the challenge of planning meals day after day.

I hope you will dive into the pasta chapter or try a different burger every week. Are you someone who likes to cook chicken? Turn to page 69 and try a few of the chicken and turkey recipes. You will find ideas and recipes you will want to re-create many times over, and your family will thank you for it.

PART OF THE ROUTINE

If you're anything like me, you probably cut recipes out of magazines, bookmark them online, and stick Post-Its throughout cookbooks. These are the recipes you want to try, that sound good and that you are pretty sure the kids will like. Some might be ambitious dishes that you fantasize making for your next dinner party, while others are far easier. Guess which ones actually get made? I'm a chef, and while it's nice to tackle the more complex recipes now and again, the recipes that are most apt to get tried in the Ponzek-Addonizio household are those that are most accessible.

Every recipe in this book falls into that category. Accessible. Easy. Often quick. Family tested. Believe me, if anything seemed like a pain when I was testing, it did not make the cut. My family and friends patiently ate their way through more than a year of trial and error, and the best, most popular results made it into the book.

I hope you find several—or more!—dishes here that resonate with you and your family. I want them to become part of your routine; I hope you will make them over and over so that before you know it, the dishes are more yours than mine. I would be honored.

THE ORGANIZATION FACTOR

I organized *The Dinnertime Survival Cookbook* to reflect how many of us cook today. Most of us have a thirty-second conversation every day that goes something like this: "What's for dinner?" "What do you feel like eating?" "What do we have in the 'fridge?"

We are as apt to say, "Let's have pasta tonight," as "Let's grill this weekend," or "I feel like a salad." It's easy to imagine them as starting points for a whole meal and so I arranged the book so that when you feel like chicken, there's a chicken chapter. If you want a sweet ending to the meal, there's a chapter with recipes for baked goods and other desserts. If your family likes eggs and pancakes for supper, go to the chapter called "Breakfast for Dinner." And if you feel like spending a lazy afternoon making a stew or braise, there is a chapter on long, slow cooking. This is how we cook nowadays, and this is how I present the food that I hope you will want to make for your family and your friends.

A FEW TIPS TO MAKE COOKING EASIER

I believe in planning ahead. Like yours, my life gets ridiculously busy, but if I take a few minutes in the morning or the night before to marinate a steak or fish fillet, I actually look forward to dinner. Same is true of chopping an onion or carrot, making a salsa, washing and drying salad greens, blanching vegetables, or measuring dry ingredients for a cake. Just a few short minutes of ahead-of-time prep make a significant difference at the end of the day. Try it once and you will see what I mean.

Despite this belief, between work, home, and the kids, I don't always take my own advice, and therefore I treasure the weeks when I sit down on Sunday afternoon or Monday morning and plan an entire week's meals. With this forethought, I am on easy street. In the end, I usually make only four or five of these planned meals, but I feel like I'm ahead of the game!

I might make a simple and quick pasta tonight and at the same time, put together a marinade for pork or beef, which we will eat tomorrow. I am always glad when I make the time to do this. As I drive home after a hectic day and remember that I have something marinating, I feel lighter. "Oh good! Dinner is just about ready." And it's true.

If I can, I nearly always measure and mix the dry ingredients for baked goods ahead of time and grill or roast extra veggies. These two very different activities save time and energy and demonstrate that with a little bit of planning, dinner is nearly done. It's waiting for you and your family.

The next two sections outline some of the things I suggest we all try to do to make it more fun and relatively effortless to cook tempting and healthful meals for our families.

SHOPPING

Make a comprehensive shopping list based on the meals you plan to make for the week. When you have the ingredients on hand, cooking is not frustrating. If you plan a week's worth of meals, understand that you may miss a meal or two. Best laid plans and all that! Still, having ingredients on hand lowers stress levels, and you can always freeze the chicken breasts or sausages for a later meal.

Before you head for the market, take a look through your pantry. Most of us could probably make several meals from the stores on those shelves. I might check the freezer in the morning and pull out some chicken breasts or pork chops that I had forgotten I had. Main course, check! Rice in the pantry, check! Now I have only to worry about a vegetable to round out the meal.

In addition to my needs for the week's meals, I try to keep the following on hand:

- **One or two extra cans of beans and tomatoes (I have always bought extra tubes of toothpaste; why not extra pantry staples?)**

- **One or two extra jars of marinara sauce**

- **An extra bottle of soy sauce and an extra bottle of hoisin, which are integral to so many marinades and sauces**

- **A few jars of roasted red peppers to use when I don't have time to roast fresh red bell peppers**

- **Extra olives to toss into salads and cooked dishes**

- The best olive oils and vinegars available (remember to store oils away from heat)

- Extra cans of quality chicken stock (freeze what you don't use for later)

- Washed salad greens in plastic bags

- Pasta, quinoa, couscous, and rice

- Pre-cut butternut squash

- Crumbled feta, goat, and blue cheeses

- Roasted chickens from reliable stores

COOKING

Always, always prepare a little more than you need. This is particularly true for foods such as vegetables, chicken, beef, and shrimp, as well as for condiments and vinaigrettes with good shelf lives. Think about how you eat. Does your family like leftovers? Make a lot of sandwiches? Like savory foods for breakfast?

When I cook I try to:
- Roast or grill extra vegetables (onions, eggplant, squash, potatoes, carrots, and mushrooms, to name a few) to eat the next day. They are great in omelets and scrambled eggs, tossed with pasta, and added to sandwiches.

- Cook more brown rice than needed and refrigerate to use for quick fried rice with veggies and tofu, chicken, shrimp, beef, or the Dinnertime Burritos on page 199.

- Freeze leftover pancakes and waffles, stacked and wrapped in plastic. This way they are ready to microwave in the morning for breakfast.

- Form hamburger patties from ground meat, wrap them individually, and keep them in the freezer.

- Double soup recipes and freeze the remaining half for later use (don't freeze soups with cream).

- Cook a second flank steak or extra chicken breasts to use for sandwiches and salads the next day.

- Freeze fresh breadcrumbs to always have them on hand.

- Make good use of marinades by mixing them in the morning and letting chicken, beef, pork, lamb, and fish soak for hours in anticipation of dinner.

- Prepare pot roasts, stews, braises, and chilis the day before. This serves two purposes: I cook when I have the time and inclination and these dishes always taste better the second day.

- Blanch and then shock green vegetables early in the day and refrigerate for later use in stir-fries, rice and pasta dishes, and soups.

- **Double recipes for condiments** that can be refrigerated for a week or more. Use them on sandwiches and with grilled or pan-seared meat and poultry to jazz up later meals.

- **Refrigerate vinaigrettes in lidded glass jars.** When needed, shake and drizzle over salads and other foods.

- **Measure the dry ingredients for baked goods ahead of time** and then mix them with the liquid ingredients just before baking. This saves time and encourages me to actually bake something wonderful. And I find I measure more accurately in the evening than early in the morning.

As a final note, as much as I like to plan ahead, I am not the kind of cook who stocks up on massive amounts of food at big box stores. I buy only two or three cans and jars of foods I like and use a lot. I don't fill a chest freezer with half a steer or dozens of chicken breasts. Frankly, I am not organized enough for such bulk shopping and storing. I know I would forget about the supplies stashed at the rear of the pantry or back of the freezer and would end up tossing dusty, rusting cans and freezer-burned meat. Many people shop this way and I admire their organizational abilities, but I am fortunate to live in a region of the country where the supermarket, farmers' market, butcher's, and fish shops are short drives from my house.

Nevertheless, a little forethought pays off and surviving the challenge of cooking every night is a lot easier and far less stressful when you plan ahead. Take my word for it.

BEYOND MUSTARD AND MAYO

When you leaf through the pages of *The Dinnertime Survival Cookbook*, you will note a number of sauces, salsas, pestos, and chutneys. These are what make eating fun and adventuresome. Anyone can grill a pork chop or chicken breast for an everyday meal, but if you team it with the Rosemary Chimichurri on page 104 or the Nectarine Chutney on page 119, it turns into something quite memorable.

I have nothing against store-bought condiments, but those you make yourself are far more flavorful, colorful, and interesting. It's well worth your time to make them often and keep them in the refrigerator. Doing so is inspirational. You'll be more eager to make a simple turkey sandwich if you know you can jazz it up with the Pineapple-Jicama Salsa on page 114 or to grill tuna for supper if you have some of the Mango Sauce on page 55 on hand. They might look new and unfamiliar to you now, but I guarantee you will come back to them time and again to dress up other foods. It's reassuring to know they are in the fridge, waiting for you to pull them out when you need them. It is a way to deepen your cooking, to make it more exciting and appealing for everyone who eats at your house. This is the kind of thing that brands you as "a good cook."

I SAID "EASY," NOT ALWAYS "QUICK"

In the end, I believe in cooking, and cooking is what this book is about. It is a skill that demands some attention to the quality of the ingredients and proficiency with certain techniques. The food you buy makes a big difference in the taste of any dish and when I think it's important to go the extra mile to insure you have the best, I will say so. When I use "exotic" ingredients for Asian or Mexican food, I try to use the same ones a few times over so that once you buy a bottle of rice wine or a can of chipotle peppers packed in adobo sauce, you can use it several times. Finally, without being tedious, I aim for precision in the recipes, paying close attention to prep instructions, heat intensity, and visual cues for doneness to insure success.

The recipes in *The Dinnertime Survival Cookbook* are easy. Sure, some are a little trickier than others, but all can be mastered by a home cook. Not every recipe is quick. I don't subscribe to the under-30-minutes style of cooking, although some of the dishes here fall into the category. For instance the Gingered Salmon Burgers on page 173, the Asian Chicken Lettuce Wraps on page 94, and the Simple Spaghetti with Arugula and Parmesan on page 154 come together in less than half an hour. I love it! Yet, I never dumb down recipes to meet this criterion. On the other hand,

nothing on the following pages requires that you spend hours in the kitchen, using every pan and bowl you own as you fuss with ingredients you have never before seen, touched, or tasted.

During the years I have cooked for my family, I have become a fan of shortcuts in the kitchen, as long as they don't compromise the flavor and integrity of a dish. For instance, there was a time when I wouldn't dream of using canned beans and would soak and then cook dried beans. I also used to cook and drain lasagna noodles. No more. I am happy to use canned, drained, and rinsed beans, and I am fanatic about no-boil lasagna sheets. As long as you cover them with sufficient sauce, they are great. Both of these marvels are terrific time-savers.

I don't wince when someone uses store-bought pie crust. I find it easy to make my own, and my recipe for a flaky crust on page 236 is not only delicious, it's close to foolproof. Still, I would rather you use store-bought than miss out on the Coconut and Lime Cream Pie on page 235.

While I don't expect you to whip up complicated sauces or pastries, to spend hours reducing veal stock, or to figure out how to use a piping bag, I hope you will pay attention to the wonderful tastes, textures, and smells that are so integral to good cooking. Most of all, I hope these recipes will make your time in the kitchen just a little more rewarding, a little more flavorful—and a lot more fun.

CHAPTER 1

EASY SOUPS AND SALADS

I AM THE FIRST TO ADMIT THAT MANY OF THE PREPARED SOUPS AVAILABLE THESE DAYS ARE WONDERFUL. After all, at Aux Délices we always offer a soup or two for takeout, and our customers are nothing but enthusiastic and grateful. As delicious as these are—and I have been known to take them home for a family supper on many occasions—there is something about making soup from scratch that is just plain satisfying. When I make my own, I usually end up centering the whole meal around the soup, adding perhaps a green salad and a loaf of bread, as well as a glass of wine for an end-of-day mellow.

I realize that I have an advantage when I make soup because I have access to homemade stock at Aux Délices. Making your own is easy but admittedly it's time-consuming, requiring that you be at home while it simmers for hours and then leaving you with a pot full of spent, boiled bones and gristle. Luckily, there are some excellent brands of stock on the market, such as Swanson Certified Organic Chicken Broth and Imagine Organic Free Range Chicken Broth, which make more than passable soups. Soups made without cream freeze beautifully—another bonus as it's easy to double a recipe and freeze the extra. As much as I love a good, hearty soup, I am equally partial to smooth, satiny ones. To achieve this lovely texture all you need is a good blender—and I prefer a blender to a food processor.

Following the soups on these pages are salads, which are accompanied by some very easy vinaigrettes. I object to being too exacting when it comes to salads, as a little more lettuce, a little less tomato, or a different kind of cheese can make a salad your own. Instead, I tempt you with the unexpected, such as the robust raw kale salad and the more fragile watermelon salad. I absolutely love the recipe that relies on shaved Brussels sprouts and once you try it, I hope you agree with me. Just about anything goes when it comes to salad.

SPICY CUCUMBER, AVOCADO, AND MANGO SOUP

For a lovely, elegant chilled soup, try this one: It's just right as a first course or a light summer lunch. The sweet mango and the fire-hot jalapeño cut the richness of the avocado for a perfect balance of flavors and a beautiful pale green hue. I like to use Greek yogurt, but any plain yogurt works well. This is a gorgeously smooth soup.

Serves 4 to 6

2 ripe avocados

2 English cucumbers, sliced

1 mango, peeled, pitted, and flesh removed

1 cup plain Greek yogurt

¼ cup chopped cilantro

Juice and grated zest of 2 limes

2 teaspoons kosher salt

1 teaspoon chopped fresh mint leaves

1 teaspoon finely diced jalapeño pepper

Freshly ground black pepper

Cut the avocados in half lengthwise and remove the pits. Scoop the avocado flesh into a large bowl.

Add the cucumbers, mango, yogurt, cilantro, lime juice, lime zest, salt, mint, and jalapeño. Add 1 ½ cups of water and stir well.

Transfer the soup to a blender. You will have to do this in two batches. Purée until smooth and return to the bowl. Cover and refrigerate for at least 2 hours or until very cold. The soup will keep for up to 3 days.

Season to taste with pepper and more salt and lime juice, if needed. Garnish with cilantro or mint leaves.

CURRIED ZUCCHINI SOUP

Everyone wonders what to do with summer's bumper crop of zucchini. The green squash overflows baskets at farmers' markets and grows like crazy in backyard gardens. This curried soup is one of the best ways I have come up with to use the somewhat mild-tasting squash. And when we offer it at Aux Délices, it's always a top seller.

Serves 8

2 tablespoons unsalted butter

2 medium-size carrots, peeled and thinly sliced

3 ribs celery, thinly sliced

1 small onion, peeled and thinly sliced

1 teaspoon curry powder

3 zucchini, trimmed and cut into large dice (about 3 pounds)

6 cups chicken or vegetable stock

½ cup heavy cream

2 teaspoons kosher salt

Freshly ground black pepper

In a large soup pot, melt the butter over medium heat and when it begins to bubble, add the carrots, celery, onion, and curry powder. Cook, stirring, for 6 to 8 minutes, or until the vegetables soften.

Add the zucchini and stock and bring to a boil. Reduce the heat and simmer for 12 to 15 minutes or until the zucchini is tender. Stir in the cream, let the soup return to a boil, and then remove it from the heat.

Transfer the soup, in batches, to a blender and process until smooth. Return the puréed soup to the pot and season with salt and pepper. Reheat, if necessary, and serve hot.

GRILLED CORN AND CHEDDAR SOUP

For a long time, I never understood the attraction of cheese soups. I loved cheese and I liked soup but didn't think the two needed to meet. That is, until I started experimenting. Cheese adds great flavor to many soups, and particularly this one with an earthiness provided by the grilled corn.

Serves 6

4 ears fresh corn, husked

5 slices bacon, cut into ½-inch pieces

2 tablespoons olive oil

1 onion, sliced

1 tablespoon all-purpose flour

4 cups chicken or vegetable stock, preferably homemade

2 medium potatoes, peeled and cut into small dice

¾ cup heavy cream

6 ounces Cheddar cheese, shredded (about 2 cups)

2 teaspoons kosher salt

Freshly ground black pepper

2 tablespoons chopped fresh chives or flat-leaf parsley

Preheat a gas or charcoal grill to medium-high.

Grill the corn for 3 to 4 minutes on each side until the corn is cooked and lightly charred and the kernels soften slightly. Set aside to cool.

When cool enough, scrape the corn kernels from the cobs. Discard the cobs.

In a large sauté pan, cook the bacon over medium heat for about 5 minutes or until crispy. Remove with a slotted spoon, leaving the fat in the pan. Add the olive oil and onion to the pan and sauté for 6 to 8 minutes, or until translucent. Sprinkle the flour over the onion and cook, stirring, for about 2 minutes.

Add the stock, potatoes, and corn kernels and bring to a boil. Reduce the heat and simmer the soup for 12 to 15 minutes, or until the potatoes are tender when poked with a fork.

Stir in the cream and cheese and cook for 5 minutes to heat through and melt the cheese. Season with salt and pepper and serve garnished with the chives or parsley.

CHILLED TOMATO SOUP

You may be familiar with hot tomato soup, specifically the famous soup sold in red and white cans from coast to coast, but if you haven't tried the real thing refreshingly cold, here's your opportunity. Make this when the tomatoes are at their best in the markets or on the vine. The soup requires zero cooking and so could not be easier. Just let the ingredients mellow in the refrigerator for a number of hours so that the juices exude from the tomatoes, and then zap everything in a blender. Done! If you have access to heirloom tomatoes, all the better. It's one of my all-time summer favorites.

Serves 4 to 6

3 pounds ripe tomatoes, cored and cut into large dice

1 cup extra-virgin olive oil

¼ cup balsamic vinegar

14 to 16 fresh basil leaves

2 teaspoons kosher salt, plus more for seasoning

2 garlic cloves, thinly sliced

Freshly ground black pepper

½ cup crème frâiche (optional)

Put the tomatoes, oil, vinegar, about 10 basil leaves, 2 teaspoons of salt, and garlic in a large glass, ceramic, or other nonreactive bowl. Stir gently, cover, and refrigerate for at least 6 hours and up to 10 hours or overnight.

Process the soup in a blender in batches. Taste and adjust the seasoning with basil, salt, and pepper.

Garnish each serving with a swirl of crème frâiche, if desired, and the remaining fresh basil leaves.

SPANISH GAZPACHO

Some folks call this white gazpacho; I call it Spanish Gazpacho because of the sherry vinegar, which should be the best you can find. Whatever your preferred moniker, please give it a try; you'll love it! Like most gazpachos, there is no cooking, no tending, no fussing. Mix everything together in a blender, season with salt and pepper, and go for it. Everyone is wowed by the unexpected flavors and refreshing coolness.

Serves 4 to 6

1 cup seedless green grapes

½ cup sour cream

⅓ cup sliced blanched almonds

3 slices white bread, crusts removed and cubed

2 cucumbers, peeled and diced

1 shallot, sliced

1½ cups cold water

⅓ cup extra-virgin olive oil

2 tablespoons sherry vinegar

2 teaspoons salt

Freshly ground black pepper

In a large mixing bowl, combine all the ingredients and stir gently to mix. Blend in batches until very smooth. Season with salt and pepper if necessary.

Process the soup in a blender in batches. Taste and adjust the seasoning with salt and pepper.

WHITE BEAN AND ARUGULA SOUP

The peppery arugula and good dose of Parmesan cheese provide just the right amount of sharpness to this lovely white bean soup, which otherwise might be a little tame for some tastes. I have always been a vocal fan of bean soups; this one is among the best I make. I usually soak the beans but if you don't have time, don't let it stop you making the soup. You'll need to cook it a little longer.

Serves 8 to 10

½ pound dried white beans (cannellini, Great Northern, and navy beans all work well)

3 tablespoons olive oil

1 onion, thinly sliced

4 ribs celery, thinly sliced

4 cloves garlic, thinly sliced

10 cups chicken or vegetable stock

3 sprigs rosemary, chopped (about 1 tablespoon)

6 ounces arugula

½ cup grated Parmesan cheese

3 teaspoons salt

Freshly ground black pepper

If you have time, put the beans in a large bowl and add enough cold water to cover by about 1 inch. Let the beans soak for at least 6 hours or overnight. Drain.

In a large soup pot heat the oil until just shimmering. Add the onion, celery, and garlic and cook for 12 to 14 minutes over medium-low heat, or until softened but not browned.

Add the beans, stock, and rosemary and bring to a boil over medium-high heat. Reduce the heat to medium and simmer for 50 to 60 minutes, or until the beans are tender.

Stir the arugula, cheese, salt, and pepper into the soup and remove from the heat.

Transfer the soup, in batches, to a blender or food processor and process until very smooth. Return the puréed soup to the pot and season with salt and pepper. Reheat, if necessary, and serve hot.

How I Learned to Use Canned Beans

Time was when I bypassed the cans of cooked beans on the supermarket shelf in favor of packages of dried beans. Hard as pebbles, dried beans usually require hydrating before they can be cooked, although I have made plenty of soups without soaking the beans. While this is an easy process, it takes time. Lately I have relaxed and started relying more and more on canned beans.

I still think the texture of beans you soak and cook yourself is slightly better than that of the beans that come from a can, but the difference is slight and in the interest of saving time and making a busy life easier, I use canned beans in most of the recipes in this book.

If you want to soak your own, please do so! (See White Bean and Arugula Soup on page 24 for a recipe that uses them.) You may have a few sacks of dried beans in the cupboard you want to use up, or you just might prefer to start "from scratch." If so, figure that $\frac{1}{2}$ cup of dried beans (black beans, kidney beans, navy beans, chickpeas) will swell to $1\frac{1}{2}$ cups after soaking and cooking. This is the equivalent of one 15-ounce can of beans. If you have a one-pound bag of dried beans, they will cook up to equal four 15-ounce cans.

How do you soak beans? Put the dried beans in a large bowl or similar container and cover them with cold water with an inch or two to spare. Let them sit in the water for at least six hours and for as long as overnight. Beans are forgiving and don't demand a lot of precision at this point.

Once the beans have soaked, at which point they will be visibly plump, drain them and put them in a large pot. Add water or stock (depends on the recipe) to cover by three or four inches (again, the amount will depend on the recipe) and bring to a boil over high heat. Skim any foam that rises to the surface, turn the heat to low, and simmer gently until soft but not mushy. The time depends on the kind of bean but most beans need between 45 and 90 minutes to cook. Lentils, split peas, and black-eyed peas don't require soaking.

BUTTERNUT SQUASH AND PEAR SOUP

When the weather turns crisp and cool in the autumn, you can find me at farmers' markets demonstrating how to make this perfect fall soup, which is always a crowd-pleaser both at the markets and Aux Délices. Everyone is mad about butternut squash soup, and this one stands out, although you can make it with other fall squashes with tasty results. The pears enhance the squash's natural sweetness and the dash of cinnamon brings it home. Just right for a chilly day. I often buy squash that's already peeled and cut to make life easier.

Serves 6 to 8

2 tablespoons unsalted butter

2 medium-size carrots, peeled and sliced

2 ribs celery, thinly sliced

1 small onion, sliced

1¼ pounds assorted fall squash, such as butternut, acorn, and Hubbard, peeled and cut into chunks

2 pears, cored and cut into large dice

6 cups chicken or vegetable stock

¼ teaspoon ground cinnamon

1 teaspoon salt

Freshly ground black pepper

In a large soup pot, melt the butter over medium heat. When the butter begins to bubble, add the carrots, celery, and onions and cook for 10 to 12 minutes, or until softened without browning.

Add the squash and pears and stir to mix with the vegetables. Add the stock and cinnamon and bring to a boil over medium-high heat. Reduce the heat and simmer for 25 to 30 minutes or until the squash is tender when poked with a fork.

Transfer the soup, in batches, to a blender and process until smooth, or blend with an immersion blender. Return the puréed soup to the pot and season with salt and pepper. Reheat, if necessary, and serve hot.

SPRING ASPARAGUS AND PEA SOUP

Looking for a way to welcome springtime? Try this agreeable soup flavored with tender, grassy asparagus and sweet peas. When I want to make this a little more sophisticated, I garnish each bowl with lump crabmeat or chopped cooked lobster. Sautéed wild mushrooms would be an elegant embellishment, too.

Serves 8

2 large leeks, trimmed, white part only

2 bunches asparagus, tips reserved and ends removed

3 tablespoons unsalted butter

½ medium-size onion, thinly sliced

2 tablespoons all-purpose flour

8 cups chicken or vegetable stock

2 cups peas, fresh or frozen

2 teaspoons salt

1 teaspoon chopped fresh thyme

Freshly ground black pepper

Split the leeks in half lengthwise and rinse under cool, running water to remove any sand or grit. Cut the leeks into ½-inch-thick half-moon slices. Slice the stems of the asparagus into pea-size pieces.

In a small pot of lightly salted water, blanch the asparagus tips over medium heat for 3 to 4 minutes, or until tender. Drain and transfer the tips to a bowl filled with ice and water for 1 minute to stop the cooking. Drain and reserve.

Melt the butter in a large soup pot over medium heat. When bubbling, cook the leeks and onion over low heat for about 10 minutes until softened but not browned. Sprinkle the flour over the vegetables and cook for about 2 minutes, stirring constantly.

Add the stock and bring the soup to a boil over medium-high heat. Skim off any residue that rises to the top and then add the asparagus pieces and the peas and simmer for 4 to 5 minutes, or until the asparagus is tender. Season the soup with salt, thyme, and pepper.

Transfer the soup, in batches, to a blender and process until smooth. Return the puréed soup to the pot and season with salt and pepper. Reheat, if necessary, and serve hot.

SWEET POTATO SALAD WITH MANGO

Want a change from typical summertime potato salad? Try sweet potato salad with fresh, juicy mango. This smoky-spicy-sweet alternative to mayonnaise-drenched potato salad is super-healthful, too.

Serves 6 ⟋⟍⟋⟍⟋⟍⟋⟍⟋⟍⟋⟍⟋⟍⟋⟍⟋⟍⟋⟍⟋⟍⟋⟍⟋⟍⟋⟍

4 medium sweet potatoes

¼ cup fresh lime juice (from 1 to 2 limes)

Kosher salt

½ cup extra-virgin olive oil

3 tablespoons adobo sauce (from a can of chipotle peppers in adobo; reserve peppers for another use)

2 tablespoons chopped fresh cilantro

Grated zest of ½ lime

1 ripe mango, peeled, pit removed, and cut into medium-size dice

3 scallions, trimmed and sliced on the bias

1 small red pepper, ribs and seeds removed, julienned

Freshly ground black pepper

Preheat the oven to 350°F.

Put the sweet potatoes on a baking pan and roast for about 1 hour, or until just fork-tender (alternatively, microwave each separately for 5 to 7 minutes on high power). The potatoes can be cooked up to 24 hours ahead of time.

Allow the sweet potatoes to cool. Peel and cut each into ¹/₂-inch dice.

Whisk together the lime juice and a sprinkling of salt until the salt dissolves. Add the olive oil and adobo and whisk well. Stir the cilantro and lime zest into the vinaigrette.

Transfer the sweet potatoes to a large serving bowl and add the mango, scallions, and red pepper. Drizzle with the vinaigrette and toss gently. Season to taste with salt and pepper and serve.

CHARRED PEPPER, TOMATO, AND SOURDOUGH BREAD SALAD

If you, like me, gravitate toward the rich, full flavor of bread soaked with a salty-tangy vinaigrette, make this salad the next time you come across really good, ripe summer tomatoes and garden-fresh basil. It's a great side salad and wonderful for company both for its rounded flavors and because it can be made ahead of time. I make this with slightly tart sourdough bread and a piquant red wine vinaigrette and then toss it with charred red peppers, a good measure of capers, and a handful of briny black olives. The last are optional but I love 'em. If you don't feel like roasting the peppers, buy roasted red peppers in jars. And try the vinaigrette on all sorts of salads. It's really good on tossed greens.

Serves 6 to 8

3 red bell peppers

3 cups cubed sourdough bread (1-inch cubes)

2 large ripe tomatoes, cored and finely diced

½ cup thinly sliced basil leaves

½ cup thinly sliced red onion

2 tablespoons drained capers

½ cup pitted black olives (optional), sliced

2 to 3 tablespoons Red Wine Vinaigrette (recipe follows on page 32)

Kosher salt and freshly ground black pepper

Preheat a gas or charcoal grill on medium heat, or preheat the broiler to char the peppers. You can also use the flame of a gas burner. Put the peppers directly on the grill or on a broiler pan, or hold with tongs over the gas flame and char on all sides, turning to blacken evenly. This will take 5 to 8 minutes in total. Transfer the charred peppers to a bowl and cover with plastic wrap for at least 10 minutes.

Preheat the oven to 350°F.

Peel the peppers (do not worry if a little blackened skin clings to the flesh) and then remove the stems and scrape out the seeds. (Do not do this under running water.) Cut the peppers into 1-inch pieces.

Spread the bread cubes on a baking sheet and toast them for about 10 minutes or until light golden brown and crispy.

In a large bowl, mix together the toasted bread, charred peppers, tomatoes, basil, onion, capers, and olives, if using. Toss with the vinaigrette and season to taste with salt and pepper.

RED WINE VINAIGRETTE

Makes about ³/₄ cup

¼ cup red wine vinegar

1 garlic clove, thinly sliced

¼ teaspoon kosher salt

½ cup extra-virgin olive oil

Freshly ground black pepper

Whisk together the vinegar, garlic, and salt until the salt dissolves. Still whisking, slowly drizzle in the olive oil until incorporated. Season to taste with pepper and serve.

If not using right away, cover and refrigerate for up to 1 week. Shake or whisk well before using.

SHAVED BRUSSELS SPROUT SALAD WITH APPLES AND PARMESAN

This salad never ceases to amaze me. I have served it to skeptical adults who swear they "hate Brussels sprouts," only to witness them dig in with gusto after the first bite. When I offer samples at farmers' markets, folks say it's lighter and tastier than expected. Even kids come back for seconds! Somewhat unusual raw salads are extremely popular these days with everyone concerned with their health, and this is one of the best. It takes only minutes to put together and the sweet-and-tart flavors of the dressing and apples mingle deliciously with the shaved Brussels sprouts and cheese, making it a true joy to eat.

Serves 6 to 8

1 teaspoon salt

¼ cup red wine vinegar

¾ cup extra-virgin olive oil

Freshly ground black pepper

1 pound Brussels sprouts

2 tart apples, preferably Rome, cored and cut into small dice

2 ounces Parmesan cheese, shredded

In a small bowl, whisk together the salt and vinegar. Slowly whisk in the olive oil until well combined. Season with pepper and set aside.

With a sharp knife, trim the bottoms of the Brussels sprouts and remove any tough outer leaves. Slice each sprout as thinly as possible, using a sharp knife or a mandolin. Transfer the sprouts to a serving bowl and add the apples and cheese.

Whisk the vinaigrette again to emulsify and toss about ¾ cup of it with the salad. Use more if needed. Taste and adjust the seasonings with salt and pepper, if needed. Serve right away.

WATERMELON, TOMATO, AND FETA SALAD

I make this salad all summer long, both at home and at Aux Délices, and it's as popular with my family as my customers. It wasn't until cookbook author Rozanne Gold was a guest on my radio show, Two Hungry Women, did I realize she had a similar idea even before I did. Thanks, Rozanne! By the way, the Lime Vinaigrette (and the lemon version on page 41) are delicious drizzled over grilled fish, chicken, and of course, fresh green salads.

Serves 6

3 cups diced seedless watermelon (1-inch dice) (from a 2-pound watermelon)

1 pint grape tomatoes, halved lengthwise

10 pitted Kalamata olives, halved

½ small red onion, thinly sliced

½ cup basil leaves cut in a chiffonade see note (page 155)

1 tablespoon chopped fresh mint

6 ounces feta cheese, crumbled or diced

½ cup Lime Vinaigrette (recipe follows), more or less to taste

Kosher salt and freshly ground black pepper

Mix together the watermelon, tomatoes, olives, onion, basil, and mint and toss gently. Add the feta and Lime Vinaigrette and toss gently. Season to taste with salt and pepper.

LIME VINAIGRETTE

Makes about ¹/₂ cup

¹/₄ cup fresh lime juice
(from 1 to 2 limes)

¹/₂ teaspoon kosher salt

¹/₃ cup extra-virgin olive oil

Freshly ground black pepper

Whisk together the lime juice and salt until the salt dissolves. Still whisking, slowly drizzle in the olive oil until incorporated. Season to taste with pepper and serve.

If not using right away, cover and refrigerate. Shake or whisk well before using.

KALE SALAD WITH FENNEL AND ALMONDS

Who would think raw kale could taste so good? Something this good for us couldn't be so wonderful, right? But it is! My customers ask for it by name, and when we make it at Aux Délices, we add whatever dried fruit or toasted nuts we have on hand. I particularly like it with the almonds and cranberries. The lemony vinaigrette is the final brilliance; it perks up the salad as nothing else can.

Serves 8

1 pound kale

1 bulb fennel, cored and very thinly sliced

1/2 cup toasted sliced almonds

1/2 cup dried cranberries

3 ounces thinly shaved Parmesan cheese

Kosher salt and freshly ground black pepper

3/4 cup Lemon Vinaigrette (page 41), more or less as needed

Stack as many of the kale leaves as you can easily handle at one time on top of each other on a cutting board. With a large sharp knife, slice them into thin strips, no more than 1/2-inch thick. Put the kale in a salad bowl.

Add the fennel, almonds, and cranberries and toss to mix. Scatter the shaved Parmesan over the salad and season to taste with salt and pepper. Sprinkle the vinaigrette over the salad, toss gently but thoroughly and serve.

FARRO SALAD WITH CORN AND ASPARAGUS

Farro is one of those grains that you try once and come back to again and again, wondering why you waited so long to work it into your family's repertoire. It's a type of wheat, very like spelt but not exactly (although in most recipes one can substitute for the other), with a pleasing nutty bite. Pair it with vegetables—those I have selected here or any of your choosing—and it makes a summer salad that could serve as a main course (although it's a terrific side salad, too). I made this on the Today Show, *explaining how this is a great stand-in for the ubiquitous pasta salad.*

Serves 6

1 cup farro

12 asparagus spears, woody stems removed

1 tablespoon olive oil

Kosher salt

Freshly ground black pepper

3 ears fresh corn, husked

4 scallions, thinly sliced, white and light green parts

½ pint cherry tomatoes, halved

3 tablespoons chopped fresh chives

Lemon Vinaigrette (see page 41)

In a saucepan, bring 4 cups of water and the farro to a boil over medium-high heat. Lower the heat and simmer for about 25 minutes or until the farro is tender. Adjust the heat to maintain the simmer. Drain well.

Meanwhile, preheat a gas or charcoal grill to medium-high heat.

Lightly drizzle the asparagus with the olive oil and grill for 3 to 4 minutes or until tender. Remove from the grill and season with salt and pepper. Cut the tips of the asparagus about 1 inch from the top and then cut the remaining stalk into ¼-inch-thick pieces.

Reduce the grill heat to medium-low and grill the corn for 5 to 6 minutes, turning to char each side lightly and cook the kernels. Set aside to cool. When cool enough, cut the kernels from the corn cobs. Discard the cobs.

In a large mixing bowl, mix together the farro, scallions, corn, asparagus, tomatoes, and chives. Toss with enough of the vinaigrette to moisten the salad. Season with salt and pepper and serve.

My Secrets for Great Vinaigrettes

Start with good oils and vinegars; they are always worth the money. This is not to say you have to invest in $40 bottles of aged balsamic vinegar or super-expensive imported olive oil, but if you take the time to find quality oils and vinegars with deep, true flavors, your vinaigrettes will reflect this care. When I use a nice, aged vinegar, its rich, mellow flavor often means I don't need as much oil. While you might already invest in good olive oil, I think it's equally essential to buy good vinegar. It's fun, too, to experience the variation in flavors, acidity, and even viscosity.

When I make vinaigrettes, I dissolve the salt in the vinegar before whisking in the oil. I find that when the vinegar is seasoned with salt before you add the oil, it's easier to taste the saltiness and determine if the dressing is properly seasoned.

Finally, after you dress the greens with the vinaigrette, season them with salt and freshly ground pepper. Many people forget this step and I find it really makes a difference in the overall flavor.

DIJON VINAIGRETTE

Makes about ³/₄ cup ⊃⊂⊃⊂⊃⊂⊃⊂⊃⊂⊃⊂⊃⊂⊃⊂⊃⊂⊃⊂⊃⊂⊃⊂⊃⊂⊃⊂⊃⊂⊃⊂

¼ cup red wine vinegar

2 tablespoons chopped shallots

½ teaspoon kosher salt

1 tablespoon Dijon mustard

½ to ¾ cup extra-virgin olive oil, or as needed

Freshly ground black pepper

In a small bowl, whisk together the vinegar, shallots, and salt until the salt dissolves. Whisk in the mustard until smooth. Slowly add the oil to emulsify the vinaigrette. You may not need all the oil. Season with pepper and serve.

If not using right away, cover and refrigerate for up to 1 week. Shake or whisk well before using.

LEMON VINAIGRETTE

Makes about ³/₄ cup ⊃⊂⊃⊂⊃⊂⊃⊂⊃⊂⊃⊂⊃⊂⊃⊂⊃⊂⊃⊂⊃⊂⊃⊂⊃⊂⊃⊂⊃⊂⊃⊂

¼ cup fresh lemon juice

1 teaspoon kosher salt

½ cup extra-virgin olive oil

Freshly ground black pepper

In a small bowl, whisk together the lemon juice and salt until the salt dissolves. Slowly add the oil to emulsify the vinaigrette. Season with pepper and serve.

If not using right away, cover and refrigerate for up to 1 week. Shake or whisk well before using.

BLUE CHEESE VINAIGRETTE

Makes about 1 1/4 cup ⊃⊂⊃⊂⊃⊂⊃⊂⊃⊂⊃⊂⊃⊂⊃⊂⊃⊂⊃⊂⊃⊂⊃⊂⊃⊂

1/4 cup champagne vinegar

1 teaspoon kosher salt

2 tablespoons mayonnaise

3/4 cup extra-virgin olive oil

1/2 cup crumbled blue cheese

Freshly ground black pepper

In a small bowl, whisk together the vinegar and salt until the salt dissolves. Whisk in the mayonnaise until smooth. Slowly add the oil to emulsify the vinaigrette and then whisk in the blue cheese. Season with pepper and serve.

If not using right away, cover and refrigerate for up to 1 week. Shake or whisk well before using.

YOGURT RANCH DRESSING

Makes about 1 cup ⊃⊂⊃⊂⊃⊂⊃⊂⊃⊂⊃⊂⊃⊂⊃⊂⊃⊂⊃⊂⊃⊂⊃⊂⊃⊂⊃⊂

1/2 cup nonfat Greek yogurt

1/2 cup low-fat buttermilk

1/2 teaspoon onion powder

1/2 teaspoon garlic powder

1/2 teaspoon kosher salt

Freshly ground black pepper

1 tablespoon chopped chives

In a small bowl, whisk together the yogurt, buttermilk, onion powder, garlic powder, and salt. Stir well and season to taste with pepper. Stir in the chives.

If not using right away, cover and refrigerate for up to 3 days. Whisk well before using.

What Makes a Salad Green?

The best salads are those made with tender lettuces grown in your own garden. But let's get real. How many of us really have a garden with enough heads of lettuce for more than a few salads? For that matter, how many of us have a garden? The next-best thing is to buy beautiful-looking leafy heads sold at farmers' markets. Barring this option, go for the best-looking lettuces in small food shops and supermarkets.

What about all those tempting plastic bags filled with mixed greens? These handy packages hold salad mixes from tender spring greens, bitter greens, and romaine hearts to traditional mesclun mix, which is usually a mélange of tender chervil, arugula, oak leaf, endive, and frisée. These are super-easy to use. Everything is done for you: the lettuce is chosen, cored, washed, and torn, ready to go right into your salad bowl to be dressed with your favorite vinaigrette. Instant salad, instant good health!

I often use these bags of greens, but I always, always wash the greens in cold water and then spin them dry in a salad spinner. While the packaging companies claim the greens are washed and ready-to-go, it's sensible to give them a good rinse. Of course, the same is true of loose heads of lettuce, whether iceberg, towering heads of romaine, or tidy little heads of hydroponically raised butter lettuce.

I intentionally have not included a recipe for a green salad. There are too many variables and too many personal likes and dislikes. Plus, they are so easy to make.

I like to mix textures and flavors, so that I will include raw kale, spinach, or bitter lettuces (endive, chicory, peppery arugula) with soft, sweet-ish red leaf, Bibb, or Boston. I also like to add other tastes: sliced scallions, shredded carrots, toasted nuts, and dried fruits, as well as the old standards: tomatoes, cucumbers, and red onion. Crisp, tart apples and ripe pears work in a lot of salads, too. I also like a little crunch: croutons, crispy onions, crispy wontons. And of course, a little cheese perks up a salad. I like crumbled blue, feta, goat, or shredded Parmesan cheese.

CHAPTER 2

THE FISH MARKET

FISH IS A TOUCHY SUBJECT FOR MANY HOME COOKS, CAUSING SO MUCH ANGST MANY PEOPLE EAT IT ONLY IN RESTAURANTS. It's hard to cook and the kids complain about it, right?

No. Not really. In fact, fish is one of the easiest foods to cook and because it goes with so many side dishes and sauces, its versatility essentially knows no end. What do they say about "plenty of fish in the sea?" I suspect there are as many ways to prepare fish as those fish in the sea!

There are two tricks to successful fish cookery. First, start with fresh, fresh, fresh fish. If it's fresh, you are half the way home. I am lucky to live near several fish markets, which I think are the best places to find impeccably fresh fish. I know not everyone has this luxury, but if there is a fish store nearby, make it part of your normal routine. Another benefit of shopping at small fish markets is that you can get to know the people behind the counter, who will steer you in the right direction.

Second, know when to substitute one fish for another. If you have your heart set on a recipe for cod but there's none fresh at the market, don't walk away. Buy another mild white fish, such as black sea bass or turbot.

This isn't to say some frozen fish isn't excellent, but its quality depends on how it was frozen and stored; it must be flash frozen when very fresh and then handled carefully so that it stays frozen.

I don't have a surefire way to get kids to try fish, but the Southwestern Salmon Tacos are a good place to start. Most children like tacos and these are full of great flavors. The chipolte sour cream packs a little heat, but that's easy to control when you serve the tacos. Leave it off, if you want. I have also made suggestions for easy sauces for salmon and urge you to try them with other fish, too. I like the speed with which I can make the Sesame-Orange Scallops and the Shrimp Scampi, and the Thai Crab Cakes are always a hit for brunch, lunch, or dinner.

SOUTHWESTERN SALMON TACOS WITH AVOCADO SALSA

For these simple tacos, made with soft flour tortillas, I rely on quickly cooked salmon fillets seasoned with avocado salsa and topped with a spicy-smooth chipotle sour cream—you can whip it up in an instant. Canned chipotle peppers are great to have in the pantry. They add vibrancy to so many dishes, and once you develop a taste for the fiery chilies, you will be hooked. As I describe on page 29, leftover peppers and adobo sauce can be frozen for later use.

Serves 4

2 avocados

2 tomatoes, cored and diced

½ cup finely diced red onion

¼ cup loosely packed chopped cilantro

Juice of 1 lemon

Kosher salt and freshly ground black pepper

4 (5- to 6-ounce) salmon fillets

¼ cup canola oil

Eight 6-inch flour tortillas

Chipotle Sour Cream (recipe follows on page 50)

Cilantro leaves, for garnish

Cut each avocado in half lengthwise and remove the pit. Carefully scoop the flesh from the shell and dice it. Toss the diced avocado with the tomato, onion, cilantro, and lemon juice. Stir to mix and season to taste with salt and pepper.

Season the salmon fillets with salt and pepper. In a medium sauté pan, heat the oil until smoking over medium-high heat and cook the salmon, fleshy sides down, for 4 to 5 minutes on each side or until cooked through. Transfer the fillets to a platter to cool slightly.

Spoon heaping tablespoons of the avocado salsa onto each flour tortilla. Gently flake each salmon fillet with your fingers or a fork. Top the tortillas with salmon, Chipotle Sour Cream, and cilantro leaves. Serve immediately.

CHIPOTLE SOUR CREAM

Makes about ¹/₂ cup

¹/₂ cup sour cream

1 canned chipotle pepper in adobo sauce, minced

2 tablespoons adobo sauce from the can

Kosher salt

Stir together the sour cream, chipotle pepper, and adobo sauce and mix well. Season to taste with salt. Serve right away or refrigerate, if not using soon.

BLACK SEA BASS WITH GINGER AND SOY

A friend who lived in New York's Chinatown passed a similar recipe to me. Her slightly more complicated dish called for steaming a whole fish and then bathing it in boiling hot ginger oil. It was amazing, to be sure, but I have simplified the method. I kept the original ginger-scallion garnish, cooked in grape seed or plain olive oil. Don't use extra-virgin olive oil for this; you need an oil with a high smoking point so it can get hot enough to cook the ginger quickly without burning.

Serves 4

4 (5- to 6-ounce) black sea bass fillets

Kosher salt and freshly ground black pepper

3 tablespoons canola oil

4 teaspoons soy sauce

¼ cup grape seed or olive oil

3 tablespoons peeled and julienned fresh ginger

4 scallions, trimmed and thinly cut on the bias, white and light green parts

Season the bass fillets with salt and pepper.

Divide the oil between two large sauté pans and heat the canola oil until smoking over medium-high heat. Cook the bass, two fillets to a pan, for 3 to 4 minutes on each side or until cooked through. Transfer the fillets to four plates. Drizzle a teaspoon of the soy sauce over each fillet.

Return one sauté pan to the heat, add the grape seed oil, and when hot, sauté the ginger for about 1 ½ minutes or until the ginger begins to crisp up. Add the scallions and cook for a few seconds longer.

Spoon the ginger-scallion mixture evenly over the fillets. Season with salt and pepper and serve right away.

EASY ROASTED SALMON

If I were to guess, I would speculate that salmon is the most popular fish of all. And for good reason. The meaty, pinkish fish has a lovely flavor that blends well with so many others, I could go on for days coming up with recipes. This is an uncomplicated method for cooking salmon simply and successfully. I've offered some ideas for sauces for the salmon, or you can eat it "as is." You won't be disappointed. Try to buy wild-caught salmon when possible. It's better for the earth and the flavor is absolutely worth it!

Serves 4

4 (5- to 6-ounce) salmon fillets, skin-on

Kosher salt and freshly ground black pepper

1 tablespoon olive oil

Preheat the oven to 400°F. Season the salmon with salt and pepper on both sides.

Heat the olive oil in a large ovenproof sauté pan over medium-high heat until it begins to smoke. Sear the salmon fillets, fleshy-sides down, for about 1 minute.

Transfer the pan to the oven without turning the fish and roast for 8 to 10 minutes or until the salmon is somewhat firm around the edges, the skin is crisp, and the interior still bright pink. Remove the pan from the oven and transfer the salmon to plates and serve. See sidebar for serving suggestions.

How to Serve Roasted Salmon or Any Other Simple Roasted Fish

- Combine olive tapenade with grated lemon zest and spoon a dollop on top of each fillet.

- Whisk Dijon mustard with honey and chopped fresh dill and drizzle over the salmon. Typically, it's two parts mustard to one part honey, but I like it spicy, so I use less honey.)

- Mix diced fresh mango or pineapple with chopped jalapeño, cilantro, lime juice, and olive oil and serve alongside the fish.

- Mix together grapefruit, lime, and orange segments. Toss them with olive oil, lemon juice, salt, and pepper. Spoon over grilled or roasted fish.

- Cut stone fruits such as plums, peaches, and nectarines into segments and grill them alongside the salmon or another fish. Lay the segments in a fine mesh grill pan or on a piece of perforated aluminum foil. Toss the grilled fruit with a little balsamic vinegar and olives oil and serve with the fish.

- Stir a little adobo sauce (from a can of chipotle peppers in adobo sauce) into plain Greek yogurt or sour cream. Taste the mixture as you add the adobo.

- Brush salmon fillets with a mixture of smooth Dijon and grainy mustard before baking.

- Mix basil pesto with grated orange zest and olive oil and spoon it over grilled fish.

- Stir thinly sliced cucumbers and chopped fresh dill with sour cream or plain Greek yogurt and serve it with grilled or roasted fish.

- Heat butter over medium heat until golden brown and then add capers and lemon juice for a quick browned butter sauce to pour over the fish.

- To marinate the fish before roasting: Mix soy sauce, chopped fresh ginger, and lime juice, pour it over the fish, and refrigerate for at least 30 minutes and up to 2 hours.

THAI CRAB CAKES WITH MANGO SAUCE

When you buy crabmeat, it's already cooked and nowadays is generally very well cleaned of shell and cartilage. This means it's ready to go: combine the sweet crab with mint, ginger, and fiery dried red pepper flakes for these irresistible crab cakes. Make these early in the day so that they are ready to pan-fry when you are ready to serve them. You'll become a hero in your own house. Everyone loves crab cakes.

Serves 6 as an appetizer; 4 as a main course

1 pound lump crabmeat, picked over for any shells or cartilage

1 cup fresh breadcrumbs (page 55)

½ cup mayonnaise

1 large egg, beaten

3 tablespoons freshly chopped mint leaves

3 tablespoons peeled and minced fresh ginger

2 tablespoons chopped cilantro

1 tablespoon grated lime zest

2 teaspoons fish sauce

1 teaspoon lime juice

1 teaspoon kosher salt

¾ teaspoon dried red pepper flakes

Freshly ground black pepper

¾ cup canola oil

¼ cup panko breadcrumbs

1 cup Mango Sauce (recipe follows)

In a medium bowl, mix together the crabmeat, breadcrumbs, mayonnaise, egg, mint leaves, ginger, cilantro, lime zest, fish sauce, lime juice, salt, and red pepper flakes. Season to taste with black pepper.

With dampened palms form the mixture into four or six patties, depending on whether you plan to serve them as an appetizer or a main course. Refrigerate the patties for at least 20 minutes to chill, and for up to 8 hours.

Pour the oil into a deep skillet and heat over medium-high heat until hot and shimmering. The oil is ready when a few breadcrumbs sizzle when dropped into it.

Spread the panko on a shallow plate and coat the patties on both sides with the crumbs, patting them so that they adhere.

Carefully put the patties in the hot oil, using a large slotted spoon. Cook for 3 to 4 minutes on each side on medium-high heat. Lift the cooked patties from the oil and drain on a plate lined with paper towels. Serve hot, with the Mango Sauce.

MANGO SAUCE

Makes about 1 cup

1 ripe mango

1 tablespoon chili-garlic sauce

1 teaspoon honey

Juice of 1/2 lime

1/4 teaspoon grated lime zest

Peel the mango and cut the flesh from the pit. Put the flesh in a food processer and add the chili sauce, honey, lime juice, and zest. Process until smooth. Taste and add more chili sauce, honey, or lime juice to taste.

Use right away or cover and refrigerate for up to a week.

It's Easy to Make Your Own Breadcrumbs

I like to use fresh breadcrumbs and don't see any advantage in using, much less buying, dried breadcrumbs, which are flavorless. It's so easy to make your own and the results are so much better. Crab cakes, meatloaf, and other preparations are lighter and tastier with fresh breadcrumbs.

You might have heard that you should use day-old or slightly stale bread for bread-crumbs, but I don't bother. I grab a few slices of bread from a loaf, tear them into pieces and then into the food processor or blender they go. Be sure you don't process them too long, as moist breads can clump together instead of forming evenly sized crumbs. Two slices of bread make about 1 cup of breadcrumbs. And if you make more than you need, they freeze well.

MISO-MARINATED COD

The flavors of miso, mirin, sake, and ginger are absolutely perfect with cod. Nobu made it famous when he served cod marinated in miso at his eponymous New York restaurant, and since then just about everyone has served one version or another. Here is mine. You'll love it. I do!

Serves 4

½ cup sake

¼ cup white miso

¼ cup mirin

2 tablespoons rice wine vinegar

2 tablespoons soy sauce

1 tablespoon finely minced ginger

2 scallions, white and light green parts, finely sliced

4 (5- to 6-ounce) cod fillets, skinned

Kosher salt and freshly ground black pepper

2 tablespoons canola oil

Stir together the sake, miso, mirin, vinegar, soy sauce, ginger, and scallions. Pour the marinade into a shallow glass dish large enough to hold the cod fillets in a single layer. Set the cod fillets in the marinade, thick, fleshy sides down. The marinade should cover the fish.

Cover the dish and refrigerate for 6 to 8 hours. Turn the fish once during marinating.

Lift the fillets from the marinade and lightly season both sides of the fish with salt and pepper.

Preheat the oven to 400°F.

Heat the oil in an oven-safe skillet over medium heat. When hot, lay the cod in the pan and let it cook for about 1 minute. Transfer the skillet to the oven. Cook for about 6 to 8 minutes or until cooked through. Serve hot.

Mini-Glossary
of Japanese Food

Miso: This fermented bean paste is most commonly sold as white, red, or black miso, although you may also see yellow miso. It's made from soy beans and rice or barley and is used as a seasoning. It falls into the category of "a little goes a long way."

Mirin: Mirin is sweetened rice wine with a very low alcohol content. Although it sometimes is called sweet sake, mirin is used as a condiment in Japanese cooking, not a wine for drinking.

Panko breadcrumbs: Delicate and crystal shaped, panko breadcrumbs originated in Japan but have migrated to just about everywhere. They form exceptionally light, crispy crusts on fried foods.

Sake: An alcohol brewed from rice, sake is sometimes called rice wine, although it's not actually wine since its production method is closer to that of beer, and it has a higher alcohol content than either wine or beer.

Rice wine vinegar: For most cooking needs, rice wine vinegar and rice vinegar can be used interchangeably. Depending on who makes it, the name is the only difference between the two.

SESAME-ORANGE SCALLOPS

I am partial to the quick sauce for this dish made with scallops or shrimp. The tangy citrus cuts the sweetness of the seafood and turns this into a pretty spectacular meal. Don't skip toasting the sesame seeds. It takes only a minute and really adds a lot of flavor.

Serves 4

2 teaspoons white sesame seeds

2 teaspoons cornstarch

2 cups orange juice

20 large sea scallops (substitute large shrimp, peeled and cleaned)

Kosher salt and freshly ground black pepper

3 tablespoons canola oil

2 tablespoons peeled, minced ginger

2 garlic cloves, minced

2 teaspoons grated orange zest (optional)

2 tablespoons soy sauce

¼ teaspoon dried red pepper flakes

2 tablespoons chopped cilantro

In a small dry pan, spread the sesame seeds in a single layer and cook over medium heat for about 1 minute, or until they turn golden brown and are fragrant. Remove from the heat and set aside to cool.

Whisk the cornstarch into the orange juice until smooth.

Season the scallops with salt and pepper.

Heat the oil in a medium sauté pan over high heat until smoking. Sear the scallops for 2 to 3 minutes on each side. Don't move them around too much, giving the scallops a chance to caramelize. (If cooking shrimp, let them cook until they turn pink.) Transfer the scallops to a serving platter and set aside.

Reduce the heat under the skillet to medium. Add the ginger and garlic to the pan and cook, stirring constantly, for about 30 seconds. Pour the orange juice mixture and orange zest, if using, into the pan and add the soy sauce and red pepper flakes. Bring to a boil over high heat and cook for 3 to 4 minutes or until the sauce is thickened and slightly reduced.

Gently stir the cilantro and reserved sesame seeds into the sauce and when nicely mixed, pour over the scallops or shrimp. Season with salt and pepper and serve right away.

Scallop Advice

Scallops may not show up on your typical shopping list and so buying them might stump you. My best advice is to buy them from a fish store or supermarket with a top-notch fish counter. Look for dry-pack scallops, which have no additives. These may feel a little sticky but won't be wet and slimy. Most of all, the scallops should smell fresh and clean, never fishy. And don't expect them to be bright white; they should look creamy or even a little bit pinkish.

ROASTED COD WITH BACON AND LEEKS

I am partial to robust, all-in-one type dishes, such as this one for cod amplified by the smokiness of bacon and the mild oniony flavor of leeks. Our cooking school director, Lynn Manheim, gave me a similar recipe that her students had loved, and I've streamlined it a little for the home kitchen.

Serves 4

4 leeks, trimmed, white parts only

2 tablespoons olive oil

4 slices bacon, cut into ½-inch pieces

Kosher salt and freshly ground black pepper

4 (5- to 6-ounce) cod fillets

¼ cup white wine

¼ cup chicken stock, preferably homemade

2 teaspoons fresh thyme leaves

Preheat the oven to 425°F.

Split the leeks lengthwise and wash them under cool, running water to remove sand and grit. Slice the leeks into half-moon slices and transfer to a bowl filled with cold water. Swish them around to clean completely. Scoop the leeks from the bowl, leaving any sand and grit on the bottom of the bowl. Drain the leeks.

Heat 1 tablespoon of the olive oil in a large, oven-safe sauté pan over high heat and cook the bacon until golden and crispy. Lift the bacon from the pan and drain on paper towels.

Add the leeks and the remaining tablespoon of oil to the pan and toss with the bacon fat. Season to taste with salt and pepper. Put the pan in the oven and roast the leeks for 15 to 18 minutes until the leeks soften. Remove from the oven.

Season the cod with salt and pepper. Add the wine, stock, and thyme to the pan and set the cod on top. Return the pan to the oven and roast for 10 to 12 minutes or until the fish is cooked through.

To serve, put the cod on four serving plates and spoon the leeks and bacon over the fish.

Don't Cry

Onions are such a familiar ingredient in so many recipes, we hardly think about them. And yet there are many kinds of onions available in the markets.

Throughout the book, I suggest using ordinary white onions, but if you have yellow onions on hand, use them instead. Both are common cooking onions and can be used interchangeably. True, white onions tend to be a little less pungent than yellow—also called a globe onion—but both sweeten when cooked.

There are other kinds of onions, too. Here are the most familiar:

Leeks are known as the most benign member of the onion family and look rather like overgrown scallions. They add a whisper of garlic to dishes, as well as a suggestion of onion, and thus are prized by many cooks for their subtlety.

Red onions are sometimes called purple onions or Bermuda onions and are sweeter and milder than either all-purpose white or yellow onions. They are most often eaten raw in salads, salsas, and relishes, and used to top sandwiches.

Scallions, which are also called green or spring onions, are immature shoots of bulb onions. Many recipes instruct you to chop up the white and light green parts of these long, slender onions and use the onions raw. Their flavor is mild and the white part can be substituted for shallots. Scallions find their way into a lot of Asian stir-fries and they are delicious grilled whole.

Shallots are one of my favorites. They look rather like a large clove of garlic and have a pleasing, mild flavor that makes them perfect for sauces and dressings.

Spanish onions are large yellow onions. Large white onions also are sometimes called Spanish onions. They usually are milder than smaller yellow onions and can be used in any recipe that calls for yellow or white onions.

Sweet onions are especially mild and juicy and are named for the region where they grow. It's the soil and climate that turns the everyday yellow globe onion into something so docile it can almost be eaten like an apple. Walla Walla, Maui, and Vidalia onions are examples of these treats, which are best served raw on sandwiches and mixed in salads.

WHOLE ROASTED RED SNAPPER WITH ROMESCO SAUCE

Roasting a whole fish is one of those undertakings that seems more complex than it actually is. I suggest a whole red snapper here, but you could just as easily roast bass or another white-fleshed fish. For me, the crowning glory is the romesco sauce, a splendid melding of roasted red peppers, tomatoes, garlic, and nuts. The sauce tastes wonderful with the fish but is equally sublime with chicken, pork, lamb—even eggs! I always make extra so that I have it in the refrigerator for a few days to render just about everything I eat much, much better. Many recipes for romesco call for whole ancho chilies, but I use ancho chili powder to make life easier. And in a pinch, jarred roasted red peppers work here, although it's not hard to roast your own.

Serves 2

1 whole red snapper, cleaned (about 2½ pounds before cleaning)

2 tablespoons olive oil

Kosher salt and freshly ground black pepper

Romesco Sauce (recipe follows)

Preheat the oven to 400°F.

Put the fish on a heavy, rimmed baking sheet so that it stands upright, as though it's swimming. Splay the belly flaps open so the fish is stable. Drizzle with olive oil and season with salt and pepper.

Transfer the baking sheet to the oven and roast for about 40 minutes or until the flesh flakes easily from the bone.

With a small, sharp knife and a fork, lift the fillets from the bones. This is easier than it sounds. Put the fillets on two serving plates. Serve with the Romesco Sauce on the side.

ROMESCO SAUCE

Makes about 2 cups

1 red bell pepper

2 tomatoes, cored and halved crosswise

2 garlic cloves, halved

¼ cup, plus 3 tablespoons olive oil

Kosher salt and freshly ground black pepper

1 slice stale bread, preferably sourdough, torn into pieces

2 tablespoons blanched almonds

2 tablespoons hazelnuts

¾ teaspoon ancho chili powder

2 tablespoons red wine vinegar

¾ teaspoon kosher salt

Preheat the oven to 400°F.

Roast the red pepper on top of the stove over a gas flame or under a broiler. Let the pepper's skin char until black on all sides, which will take about 10 minutes total. Put the charred pepper in a bowl and cover with plastic wrap. Let the pepper cool for 10 to 15 minutes.

Set the tomatoes in a shallow baking pan, top with the garlic, drizzle with 1 tablespoon of the olive oil, and season with salt and pepper. Roast for about 30 minutes or until the tomatoes shrink a little and soften. They should look somewhat collapsed.

Meanwhile, lift the pepper from the bowl and scrape off the charred skin. Remove the seeds and cut or tear the pepper's flesh into chunks.

In a medium sauté pan, heat 2 tablespoons of the olive oil over medium-high heat and cook the bread and nuts for 1 to 2 minutes, stirring, or until the nuts begin to turn golden. Lower the heat, add the red pepper and chili powder, and cook for about 1 minute longer.

Put the tomato and garlic in a food processor with any juice that has accumulated during roasting. Add the bread, nut mixture, vinegar, salt, and remaining ¼ cup of olive oil. Process until nearly smooth; the sauce should have a nubby consistency. Serve warm or at room temperature.

The sauce can be made ahead of time and refrigerated for up to 2 days.

BRONZINO VERACRUZ

This is a surprisingly easy fish dish with a great-tasting sauce that requires very little effort once you gather the ingredients. It goes beautifully with bronzino but can also be made with other firm-fleshed, white fish such as black sea bass, wild bass, and cod. And the sauce does very well made up to 24 hours ahead of time.

Serves 4

3 tablespoons olive oil

1 large onion, finely diced

6 garlic cloves, sliced

1 (28-ounce) can plum tomatoes

1/2 cup white wine

1/4 cup golden raisins

2 pickled jalapeño peppers, roughly chopped

2 tablespoons pickled jalapeño brine

2 tablespoons drained capers

2 teaspoons dried oregano

2 bay leaves

One 3-inch sprig rosemary

Kosher salt and freshly ground black pepper

4 (5- to 6-ounce) bronzino fillets

1/4 cup chopped flat-leaf parsley

Heat the oil in a large sauté pan over medium-high heat until shimmering. Reduce the heat to medium and cook the onion and garlic, stirring, for 10 to 12 minutes or until the onions soften. Add the tomatoes and their juice, crushing them with your hands or a wooden spoon as you do. Add the wine, raisins, jalapeños and brine, capers, oregano, bay leaves, and rosemary and bring to a simmer over medium-low heat. Cook for about 20 minutes, adjusting the heat to maintain the gentle simmer. Remove the bay leaves and rosemary and season to taste with salt and pepper. (Cover and refrigerate for up to 1 day if you're not eating right away. Reheat the sauce before proceeding.)

Season the bronzino with salt and pepper and then lay the fish in the sauce. Spoon 2 or 3 tablespoons of sauce over the fish and cook over medium heat for 4 to 5 minutes, or until the fish is cooked through (cooking time will vary depending on the size of the fish fillets).

Lift the fillets from the sauce and transfer to four serving plates. Spoon the sauce over the fish and sprinkle with parsley. Serve immediately.

MY HUSBAND'S SHRIMP SCAMPI

My husband makes this now and then, and I absolutely love it—and not just because I don't have to cook. It's fantastic with just the lightest coating of sauce on the shrimp and is an easy, super-quick meal that you can prepare at the end of even the busiest days. And we do! While you can dredge the shrimp in any kind of flour, if you can, use Wondra for dredging. It's less likely to clump.

Serves 4

1½ pounds shelled large shrimp

Kosher salt and freshly ground pepper

¼ cup all-purpose flour (Wondra brand works well)

3 tablespoons olive oil

2 large garlic cloves, minced

⅓ cup white wine

½ cup chicken stock, preferably homemade

2 tablespoons lemon juice (from about ½ lemon)

1 tablespoon unsalted butter

2 tablespoons chopped flat-leaf parsley

Season the shrimp with salt and pepper and toss with flour just to coat lightly. Shake off any excess.

In a large sauté pan, heat the oil until shimmering over medium heat and cook the garlic for about 30 seconds. Raise the heat, add the shrimp in an even layer, and cook for about 1 ½ minutes. Turn the shrimp over and cook for another minute or just until the shrimp begin to turn opaque.

Add the wine, stock, and lemon juice and cook for about 1 minute. Swirl the butter into the sauce and cook until it melts and is incorporated. Season to taste with salt and pepper. Sprinkle with chopped parsley and serve right away.

CHAPTER 3

IF YOU LOVE CHICKEN

MOST SHOPPERS TOSS CHICKEN INTO THEIR CARTS AS READILY AS CARTONS OF MILK AND LOAVES OF BREAD. It's a staple in many households, having reached parity with beef in terms of consumption, and by now is threatening to supplant it. We appreciate its versatility. Doesn't it go with just about everything? Without question, chicken, turkey, and even duck are easy to cook and don't break the bank.

So, aren't you ready for some new ideas for this family favorite? Read on! In this chapter, I have a recipe for roasting a whole chicken, one of the easiest and most delicious ways to prepare it. If you've not done it before, don't wait! It's ridiculously simple, absolutely delicious, and fills the house with warm, welcoming aromas. There also are quick-and-easy recipes on the following pages perfect for weekday meals, such as the Asian Chicken Lettuce Wraps (my family's top choice) and Chicken Piccata. Turkey is marketed all year long, not just during the winter holidays, and because you can buy turkey parts and ground turkey, it's increasingly appealing to home cooks. Try my Turkey Meatballs or Turkey and Sausage Meatloaf to get a taste of its flexibility. I couldn't leave out a recipe for duck; it's one of my all-time favorites and this one for Pan-Roasted Duck with Cherry Sauce is easy to make and yet fancy enough for company.

THE PERFECT ROASTED CHICKEN

If I had to choose only one way to cook chicken for the rest of my life, this would be it. As anyone in my family will confirm, this is my "go-to" method when I feel like a warm, comforting, and easy meal. Just put the whole bird in a hot oven and walk away for about an hour. Done! For whatever reason, some people are nervous about cooking a whole chicken, but there is no need for trepidation. I have tried all the techniques various people have put forth, from starting in a very hot oven to turning the breast on its side. My verdict? The approach I describe here is the most reliable and produces a golden brown bird with crisp skin and moist, tempting meat. Plus, as it roasts, the kitchen fills with cozy aromas.

Serves 2 to 3

1 (3 ½-pound) chicken

1 tablespoon unsalted butter, at room temperature

Kosher salt and freshly ground black pepper

Remove the gizzards from the chicken and reserve for another use. Lightly rinse the chicken, inside and out, and pat dry with paper towels, or let the chicken air dry if you have time. If the chicken has been refrigerated, let it come to room temperature on the kitchen counter for about 1 hour.

Position an oven rack so that it is in the center of the oven. Preheat the oven to 375°F.

Rub the chicken with the butter and season generously with salt and pepper.

Put the chicken, breast side up, in a small roasting pan or dish, just large enough to hold it comfortably but not so big that it "swims" in the pan. Roast the chicken on the center rack for about 1 hour. Rotate the roasting pan once during roasting to ensure the chicken browns evenly.

When the chicken is done, its juices will run clear when the meat is pierced with a fork, and the internal temperature of the thigh will be 180°F. Allow the chicken to rest for about 10 minutes before carving.

Flavorful Rubs and Butters and How to Use Them

One of the easiest and surest ways to add flavor to roast chicken is to rub it with a mixture of spices and other seasonings. The following rub and herb butter were developed for a three-pound chicken, but you could adapt either for just about any piece of poultry.

When you use a rub, don't be shy about working it into the poultry skin. If you let it sit on the chicken for a few minutes or even longer, the flavors just get better. If you have no time for this, pop the rubbed bird in the oven and wait for perfection!

When it comes to a flavored butter, start with good, softened butter and rub it over the chicken or press it between the bird's skin and breast meat—loosen the skin first with your fingers. This is a little messy, especially if you have never done it before, but the oozing butter lusciously mingles with the herbs to flavor the chicken deliciously as it roasts.

BROWN SUGAR CHILI RUB

Makes about 3 tablespoons

3 tablespoons light brown sugar

2 teaspoons chipotle chili powder

1 teaspoon kosher salt

1/2 teaspoon ground cinnamon

1/2 teaspoon ground cumin

1/8 teaspoon (or a small pinch) cayenne

Mix all the ingredients together and then rub over the chicken. Proceed with the recipe for roasting the chicken (but don't use any more salt, even if the recipe calls for it; there is ample salt in the rub).

SAGE-ROSEMARY HERB BUTTER

Makes about ¼ cup ⋙⋘⋙⋘⋙⋘⋙⋘⋙⋘⋙⋘⋙⋘⋙⋘⋙⋘⋙⋘⋙⋘

6 sage leaves, roughly chopped

Grated or minced zest of ½ lemon

3 tablespoons unsalted butter, at room temperature

6 sprigs fresh thyme, chopped

2 sprigs fresh sage, chopped

2 sprigs fresh rosemary, chopped

Kosher salt and freshly ground black pepper

½ head garlic (about 5 whole cloves)

Mix together the chopped sage leaves, zest, and 2 tablespoons of the butter. Put half of the butter mixture under the skin on each side of the breast, pressing it gently into the meat.

Mix the remaining tablespoon of butter with the thyme, sage, and rosemary and spread the butter over the chicken. Season generously with salt and pepper.

Put the chicken in a roasting pan and insert the garlic cloves in the cavity. Proceed with the recipe for roasting the chicken.

Do's and Don'ts
for Perfect Roast Chicken

Do:

• Start with a premium bird, the best you can afford to buy. I suggest you buy chicken marketed as organic, free-range, or pasture-raised, and hormone-free. You can find them at butchers, some supermarkets, and many farmers' markets. It really makes a significant difference in taste and texture, and you'll feel better eating a chicken that was raised right.

• Rotate the chicken halfway through cooking to ensure even browning. Cook the chicken in a pan that holds it easily without crowding but that is not too large, either. This keeps the juices nice and close to the bird, which helps keep the meat moist.

• Be sure to save any of the drippings that have accumulated during roasting and serve them with the chicken. This may be only be a few spoonfuls, but those spoonfuls will have great flavor.

Don't:

• Don't roast at too low a temperature. If you do, the chicken will look kind of blonde and the skin won't be crispy.

• Don't start with a wet bird or the skin won't brown well.

• Don't go straight from the fridge to the oven. Give the chicken time to shake off the chill (at least 45 minutes to an hour at room temperature) to ensure even cooking.

How to Carve
a Roasted Chicken

Place the bird, breast side up, on a large cutting board, preferably one that's rimmed to catch the juices.

Using a sharp carving knife, slice between the leg and the breast until you reach the joint. Use the knife to separate the thigh enough so that you can see the joint. Slice through it.

To separate the thigh from the drumstick, find the knee joint by slightly bending the leg. Cut through the joint of each leg.

Remove the wings by cutting into the joint where they're attached to the backbone.

Slice all the way through the breast along one side of the backbone, separating the breast from the spine. Repeat with the other side.

BASIL AND GOAT CHEESE–STUFFED CHICKEN WITH ROASTED TOMATO VINAIGRETTE

If you're looking for an easy way to dress up some boneless, skinless chicken breasts, look no further. If your knife is sharp, it's easy to make a small pocket in the side of the breasts and then, with your fingers, push a few tablespoons of goat cheese inside. And the good news is, it's quite impressive. Make this for a special family meal or on a night when you feel like creating a little fuss. If the goat cheese mixture gets too soft to work with, divide it into portions and freeze them for about 15 minutes so that they can firm up. I like this with the tomato vinaigrette, but you could also serve it with the Basil Pesto on page 151, or any pesto you particularly like.

Serves 4

4 ounces goat cheese

1/3 cup chiffonade of fresh basil leaves

Kosher salt and freshly ground black pepper

4 (6-ounce) boneless, skinless chicken breasts

2 tablespoons canola oil

Roasted Tomato Vinaigrette (recipe follows)

Preheat the oven to 350°F.

In a small bowl, mix together the goat cheese and basil until the herb is well incorporated in the cheese. Season to taste with salt and pepper.

With a sharp boning knife, cut a slit deep in the side of the chicken breast to make a pocket. Gently push the pocket open with your fingers and carefully stuff about 2 tablespoons of the goat cheese into each pocket. Lightly sprinkle the chicken breasts with salt and pepper.

In a large, oven-safe sauté pan, heat the 2 tablespoons of oil over high heat until smoking and cook the chicken on each side for about 1 minute, until just golden. Transfer the pan to the oven and cook for 18 to 20 minutes or until cooked through.

Remove the pan from the oven, turn the chicken breasts over and then remove them from the pan. Serve with the vinaigrette spooned over the breasts.

ROASTED TOMATO VINAIGRETTE

Makes ³/4 cup

12 cherry tomatoes

¹/4 cup olive oil

12 pitted black olives

1 teaspoon fresh chopped thyme

1 teaspoon grated lemon zest

Kosher salt and freshly ground black pepper

Split about half of the cherry tomatoes and leave the rest whole.

In a small sauté pan, heat the olive oil over medium-low heat and when hot, cook the tomatoes for about 5 minutes, or until they soften. Add the olives, thyme, and zest.

Remove from the heat and season to taste with salt and pepper. Set aside, covered to keep warm.

PARMESAN AND CORNMEAL– CRUSTED CHICKEN BREASTS

This is one of those family-friendly recipes that is as versatile as the day is long. Serve it as it is, with pasta tossed with marinara sauce, over a crisp green salad, or sliced for a wrap. You could even turn this into chicken parm. What could be better, you ask? The chicken can be breaded early in the day and refrigerated, so you'll save time when it's time to cook.

Serves 6 to 8

2 pounds boneless chicken breasts or cutlets, cut into 8 pieces

Kosher salt and freshly ground black pepper

½ cup all-purpose flour

2 large eggs, beaten

½ cup cornmeal

½ cup grated Parmesan cheese

Canola oil, for frying

Preheat the oven to 375°F.

If using chicken breasts (instead of cutlets), lay them between sheets of plastic wrap and pound with a meat mallet or the flat side of a small, heavy skillet until they are about 1 ¼-inches thick. Lightly season the chicken pieces with salt and pepper.

Put the flour in a shallow bowl and the eggs in a second shallow bowl. Mix together the cornmeal and Parmesan cheese in a third bowl.

Dip the chicken pieces first in the flour, shaking off any excess. Dip the coated chicken in the egg and then the cornmeal mixture. Transfer the coated chicken to a platter or tray until ready to cook. If you don't plan to cook the chicken for several hours, refrigerate it. Let the pieces come to room temperature before frying.

Pour the oil in a large sauté pan to a depth of about ½ inch. Heat the oil over medium-high heat until it is shimmering hot. You will know it is hot enough if you sprinkle it with a few droplets of water and it sizzles.

Using a slotted spoon, put the chicken pieces in the pan. Do not crowd the pan but instead cook the chicken in batches, if necessary. Cook the chicken for 2 to 3 minutes on each side, or until golden brown. Transfer the chicken to a sheet pan and bake for 10 to12 minutes or until cooked through. Serve right away.

ROASTED CHICKEN ENCHILADAS

This is a family classic: I've made it for my kids many times over the years and have learned a few things. First, this is great for a weekday supper and even for a football party. Next, when you use 8-inch tortillas, the portions are happily generous and the rolled enchiladas fit nicely in a single 13 x 9 x 2-inch baking dish. For smaller servings, the 6-inch tortillas work very well, but they might not all fit in the same dish. You can use tortillas right out of the package, or go the extra step to prepare the Enchilada Tortillas I describe on page 83. (They really do make a delicious difference.) This is an easy meal if you make the sauce ahead of time. You can even roll the enchiladas earlier in the day and then assemble the final casserole in the blink of an eye—well, maybe a few blinks, but you get the idea.

Serves 8 to 10

3 (8-ounce) boneless chicken breasts

Kosher salt and freshly ground black pepper

3 tablespoons olive oil

1 Spanish onion, diced

3 garlic cloves, sliced

1 red bell pepper, seeded and diced

1 large chipotle pepper in adobo sauce, chopped, plus 1 teaspoon of the adobo sauce

1½ teaspoons ground cumin

1 (29-ounce) can tomato purée

(continued)

Preheat the oven to 375°F.

Arrange the chicken in a shallow baking pan and season with salt and pepper. Bake for 20 to 25 minutes, or until just cooked through. Remove from the oven and let the chicken cool. When cool enough to handle, shred the meat with your fingers and two forks and set aside. Be sure to shred the chicken into small, fine pieces.

In a medium saucepan, heat the olive oil over medium heat until shimmering. Add the onion, garlic, red pepper, and chipotle and sauté for 10 to 12 minutes, or until the vegetables soften. Add the cumin and sauté for another minute. Add the tomato purée and chicken stock, bring to a boil, reduce the heat, and simmer for about 15 minutes. Adjust the heat up or down to maintain the simmer.

Working in batches, purée the sauce until smooth. Set aside to cool.

Toss the shredded chicken with about 3/4 cup of the cooled sauce and 2 cups of Cheddar cheese. Season with salt and pepper.

2 cups chicken stock, preferably homemade

3 1/2 cups shredded Cheddar cheese (about 10 1/2 ounces)

6 (8-inch) or 10 (6-inch) plain flour tortillas or Enchilada Tortillas (recipe follows)

Fresh cilantro, for garnish, optional

Reduce the oven heat to 350°F. Lightly spray a 13 x 9 x 2-inch baking dish with vegetable oil spray.

Put a loose cup of filling in each tortilla and roll the tortilla and transfer to the prepared pan. Repeat until all of the tortillas have been filled. If you use the smaller tortillas, you will need two pans. If you use the larger tortillas, they will fit perfectly in the single pan.

Ladle about 3 cups of the sauce over the rolled tortillas and top with the remaining cheese. Bake for about 35 to 40 minutes or until the cheese is golden brown and bubbly. Garnish with fresh cilantro, if desired.

ENCHILADA TORTILLAS

Makes 6 to 10 tortillas

5 large eggs

Kosher salt and freshly ground pepper

3 tablespoons unsalted butter

6 (8-inch) or 10 (6-inch) flour tortillas

Beat the eggs in a wide shallow bowl and season them with salt and pepper.

Heat about 1/2 tablespoon of the butter over medium heat in a nonstick skillet large enough to hold a tortilla spread out and lying flat.

Dip a tortilla in the egg wash to coat both sides. Cook for 30 to 40 seconds on each side or until light golden brown. Transfer to the skillet to cook, making sure the tortilla is spread out flat.

Repeat with the remaining tortillas, adding more butter as needed. You can stack the tortillas on top of each other as long as they are spread out as flat as possible. When cool, use as you would any tortilla.

TURKEY MEATBALLS

I married into an Italian family and have come to appreciate the Sunday tradition of pasta and meatballs. When I make meatballs at home, I often use ground turkey instead of beef and pork. Everyone loves them; they are so rich and flavorful. This is one of those recipes with a lot of ingredients, but don't let that scare you. The meatballs come together very easily: simmer them in your favorite marinara sauce for half an hour and serve over cooked pasta.

Serves 6 to 8 (makes about 18 meatballs)

2 tablespoons olive oil

1/2 large Spanish onion, finely diced (about 1/2 cup)

1/2 red bell pepper, seeded and finely diced

1/2 cup whole milk

2 large eggs, lightly beaten

3 slices white or wheat bread, crusts removed, cut into 1-inch cubes

1 1/2 teaspoons chopped fresh rosemary

1 teaspoon chopped fresh thyme

2 tablespoons chopped flat-leaf parsley

3/4 teaspoon dried oregano

2 garlic cloves, minced

1 pound ground turkey

1/2 cup grated Parmesan

1 1/2 teaspoons kosher salt

Freshly ground black pepper

Preheat the oven to 350°F. Lightly coat a baking sheet with neutral vegetable oil, such as canola oil.

Heat the olive oil in a medium skillet over medium-high heat. When hot, sauté the onions and peppers for about 5 minutes or until softened.

Meanwhile, put the milk, eggs, and bread cubes in a large mixing bowl and add the rosemary, thyme, parsley, oregano, and garlic. Add the sautéed vegetables and let the mixture sit for 3 to 4 minutes or until the bread absorbs most of the liquid.

Add the turkey, cheese, and salt and season to taste with pepper. Stir to mix well.

Dampen your palms and roll the turkey mixture into 18 meatballs, each about 2 inches in diameter. Set the meatballs on the baking sheet, leaving a little space between each one. Bake for 15 to 18 minutes or until cooked through.

TURKEY AND SAUSAGE MEATLOAF

The word that springs to mind when I think of the flavor combination of turkey, sausage, apples, and sage is "heavenly." Yes, this is a lowly meatloaf, but the melding of these flavors carries it to celestial heights. Try it; you'll see!

Serves 8

2 tablespoons unsalted butter

2 celery stalks, trimmed and minced

½ onion, peeled and cut into very small dice

3 slices white or whole wheat bread, torn into pieces

½ cup milk

1 pound ground turkey, dark meat if possible

8 ounces pork sausage, casing removed (if any) and broken into pieces

2 large eggs, lightly beaten

1 Granny Smith or Rome apple (or other tart baking apple), peeled and grated

1 tablespoon, plus 1 teaspoon chopped fresh sage

1 teaspoon kosher salt

Freshly ground black pepper

Preheat the oven to 350°F.

Melt the butter in a medium saucepan over medium-high heat until bubbling. Sauté the celery and onion for 6 to 7 minutes or until softened. Remove from the heat and set aside to cool.

In the bowl of an electric mixer fitted with the paddle attachment, beat the bread and milk on medium speed until the milk is absorbed and the mixture looks mealy.

Add the turkey, sausage, eggs, apple, sage, and sautéed vegetables and add salt and pepper to taste. Mix well on medium-high speed for 1 to 2 minutes or until the meatloaf mixture is smooth.

Transfer the meat mixture to a 9 x 5-inch loaf pan. Push the meat mixture into the corners of the pan and smooth the top. Bake for 42 to 45 minutes or until the meatloaf is cooked through. Serve hot.

CHICKEN CACCIATORE

I learned to make this from my Italian husband, Greg, and have now decided it's one of my family recipes. I make it with chicken thighs, which are an underutilized part of the bird and yet are so full of flavor and easy to find. If you prefer, you could use other chicken parts.

Serves 4

8 boneless, skinless chicken thighs

Kosher salt and freshly ground black pepper

5 garlic cloves

2 tablespoons olive oil

1 medium-size onion, thinly sliced

1 teaspoon dried oregano

1/4 teaspoon dried red pepper flakes

1 (28-ounce) can crushed plum tomatoes

2 tablespoons drained capers

1 red bell pepper, seeded and thinly sliced

1 yellow bell pepper, seeded and thinly sliced

8 ounces whole white mushrooms, sliced

1/2 bunch flat-leaf parsley, chopped (about 1/2 cup)

Lightly season the chicken thighs with salt and pepper. Slice two of the garlic cloves and leave the remaining three whole.

In a large, deep sauté pan, heat the oil over medium-high heat until it begins to smoke. Sear the chicken thighs on one side for 1 to 2 minutes, or until golden brown. Turn over and add the whole and sliced garlic with the onion, oregano, and red pepper flakes. Sauté the entire mixture for 2 to 3 minutes until the onions are light golden brown.

Add the crushed tomatoes and capers and bring to a simmer. Loosely cover the pan and cook over medium heat for about 10 minutes or until the sauce is slightly thickened.

Lay the peppers and mushrooms on top of the chicken, partially cover the pan and cook for 10 to 12 minutes, or until the peppers are tender. Do not stir.

Remove the cover, raise the heat slightly, and cook for an additional 5 to 6 minutes until the sauce's flavors come together and the chicken is cooked through. Add the chopped parsley, season with salt and pepper, and serve.

CHICKEN AND BISCUITS

Maybe it's because I spent a little of my childhood in the South that I am so crazy about buttermilk biscuits. I also love chicken pot pie and so decided to introduce these two great loves to each other for an incredible riff on a classic chicken pie. The filling is wonderfully creamy but without a drop of cream and tastes fantastic with the biscuits. If you don't feel like baking biscuits, serve the chicken filling over rice—but I hope you will try it with the biscuits because it's a treat.

Serves 6

2 pounds boneless skinless chicken breasts or a mixture of breasts and boneless thighs

4 cups chicken stock, preferably homemade

6 ounces fresh, unpeeled pearl onions or frozen pearl onions

½ cup (1 stick) unsalted butter

2 carrots, peeled and cut into small dice

3 ribs celery, cleaned and cut into small dice

½ medium onion, peeled and cut into small dice

¼ cup all-purpose flour

1 potato, peeled and cut into small dice

1 cup frozen peas, thawed for a few minutes

¼ bunch flat-leaf parsley, chopped (about ¼ cup)

Kosher salt and freshly ground black pepper

6 freshly baked Easy Buttermilk Biscuits (recipe follows on page 90)

Put the chicken and chicken stock in a large saucepan or pot. Bring to a boil over medium-high heat, reduce to a simmer, and cook for about 15 minutes or until the chicken is cooked through. Turn chicken over once or twice as it cooks. Strain stock and reserve.

Let the meat cool and when you can handle it comfortably, shred it with your fingers and set aside.

Meanwhile, bring a small pan of water large enough to hold the onions comfortably to a boil over medium-high heat. Blanch the onions for 2 minutes, drain, and then submerge the onions in a bowl of ice water to cool. After 1 to 2 minutes, remove the onions and peel them.

In a large sauté pan, melt the butter over medium heat. Add the carrots, celery, and diced onion and cook for about 10 minutes or until the vegetables are tender. Stir the flour into the vegetables and cook, stirring constantly, for 2 to 3 minutes. Slowly add the strained stock, stirring to incorporate it into the flour mixture. Bring to a boil and then reduce the heat to a simmer. Add the potatoes and peeled pearl onions and cook until tender, 12 to 15 minutes.

Finally, add the chicken and cook for about 5 minutes or until heated through. Add the peas, let them heat through, add the parsley, and season with salt and pepper.

Split the biscuits in half and put the bottom half in a large ramekin or on a plate. Spoon the chicken mixture over the biscuit bottom then place the top of the biscuit on the chicken mixture.

EASY BUTTERMILK BISCUITS

Makes 10 biscuits

3 cups all-purpose flour

2 tablespoons sugar

4 1/2 teaspoons baking powder

1/2 teaspoon baking soda

3/4 teaspoon kosher salt

1 cup (2 sticks) cold, unsalted butter, cut into small, pea-size pieces

1 1/4 cups cold buttermilk

Preheat the oven to 400°F.

In the bowl of an electric mixer with the paddle attachment, mix together the flour, sugar, baking powder, baking soda, and salt.

Turn off the mixer and add the butter all at once. Mix on medium-low speed until the dough is coarse and crumbly, with pea-size pieces of butter still visible. Don't overmix when the butter becomes crumbly, or the biscuits will be heavy and dense.

Add the buttermilk all at once and mix until the dough just comes together. Turn the dough out onto a floured counter and knead two to three times (no longer) to bring the dough together into a smooth mass.

Roll the dough out so that it is about 3/4-inch thick. Using round, 3-inch cutters, cut out 10 biscuits. Gently pat any excess into another biscuit. Transfer the biscuits as they are cut to an ungreased baking sheet. Bake for about 25 minutes or until the biscuits are golden brown and baked through. Serve hot.

SPICED APRICOT CHICKEN

As mouth-watering as this is on its own, this makes an even better, complete meal when paired with the Golden Almond Couscous on page 224. With or without the couscous, it's slightly sweet, slightly spicy, and totally appealing. The lemon and cilantro brighten up the glaze and hit it out of the park.

Serves 4

8 pieces bone-in chicken, from 1 (4-pound) chicken

Kosher salt and freshly ground black pepper

4 tablespoons olive oil

1 large onion, chopped

3 garlic cloves, finely chopped

1 tablespoon peeled and grated ginger

½ teaspoon turmeric

1 teaspoon curry powder

1 teaspoon chili powder

½ teaspoon sweet paprika

1 cup chicken stock, preferably homemade

½ cup apricot preserves

½ cup chopped dried apricots

1 teaspoon grated orange zest

Juice of ½ lemon

2 to 3 tablespoons chopped cilantro, for garnish

If using legs and breasts, cut the breasts in half; separate the thigh from the leg by cutting between the joint. Remove the thigh bone, if preferred. Lightly season the eight pieces of chicken with salt and pepper.

Heat 2 tablespoons of the oil in a heavy skillet over high heat just until smoking.

Working in batches, sear the chicken pieces on all sides, 3 to 4 minutes per side. Do not crowd the pan and reserve the seared chicken on a platter.

When the chicken is seared, pour the remaining 2 tablespoons of oil into the pan and cook the onions and garlic over medium-low heat for 2 to 3 minutes. Stir in the ginger, turmeric, curry, chili powder, and paprika.

Return the seared chicken and any accumulated juices to the skillet. Add the stock and bring to a boil over high heat. Reduce the heat to medium-low, cover, and simmer for about 15 minutes. Adjust the heat up or down to maintain a gentle simmer.

Turn the chicken over, add the apricot preserves, apricots, orange zest, and lemon juice and cook uncovered for about 15 minutes, until the sauce has thickened slightly and the chicken is tender and cooked through. Stir in the cilantro and serve.

CHICKEN PICCATA

One of the best ways to cook boneless chicken breasts is quickly in a sauté pan and once done, make an easy, fast sauce in the same pan to drizzle over the meat. Lemon and capers is a classic pairing and makes a lovely sauce, even for a quick weekday meal. When you pound the chicken, it's so much lighter and more tender—but don't bang the heck out of it. I make this all the time and never hear any complaints.

Serves 4

4 (6-ounce) boneless, skinless chicken breast halves

Kosher salt and freshly ground black pepper

All-purpose flour, for coating

½ cup canola oil

1 cup white wine

½ cup chicken stock, preferably homemade

Juice of ½ lemon

2 tablespoons cold unsalted butter, cut into small pieces

2 tablespoons drained capers

2 tablespoons chopped flat-leaf parsley

Lay the chicken breasts between two sheets of plastic wrap and pound with a meat mallet or the flat side of a small skillet until they are ¼- to ½- inch thick. Season the chicken breasts on both sides with salt and pepper and then dip in the flour to coat lightly. Shake off any excess flour.

Heat the oil in a large sauté pan over medium heat until shimmering and cook the chicken for 3 to 4 minutes on each side or until cooked through. (The time will depend on the thickness of the chicken.) You may have to do this in two batches. Transfer the chicken to a warm platter and set aside, covered, to keep warm.

Discard any oil still in the pan. Add the wine, chicken stock, and lemon juice and bring to a boil over high heat, scraping the bottom of the pan to release any browned bits. Cook for about 5 minutes and then reduce the heat to medium. Swirl the butter into the sauce and then stir in the capers. When the butter is incorporated, stir the parsley into the sauce, spoon it over the chicken, and serve right away.

LEMON-ROSEMARY CHICKEN BREASTS

When it comes to flavor, these chicken breasts are not shy. They literally are stuffed with lemon, garlic, and rosemary, and as they bake, they fill the kitchen with a heady fragrance. All each chicken breast needs is a good douse of extra-virgin olive oil for serving.

Serves 4

4 split bone-in chicken breast halves with the skin

3 lemons, thinly sliced

12 garlic cloves, thinly sliced

8 sprigs fresh rosemary

¾ cup olive oil

Kosher salt and freshly ground black pepper

Extra-virgin olive oil, for drizzling

Loosen the skin of each chicken breast by inserting your fingers between the skin and the meat. Slide 2 lemon slices, 1 whole clove of sliced garlic, and 1 sprig of rosemary under the skin of each breast.

Arrange the breasts in a shallow glass, ceramic, or other non-reactive dish and pour the oil over the chicken.

Remove the rosemary leaves from the remaining four sprigs of rosemary and scatter the rosemary leaves and remaining lemon and garlic slices over the chicken. Cover the dish and refrigerate for 6 to 8 hours or overnight.

Preheat the oven to 375°F.

Without removing the lemon slices on top of the chicken breasts, transfer the breasts to a clean baking pan. (The lemon slices are delicious once cooked, so you don't want to miss them by discarding them before roasting.) Season lightly with salt and pepper and roast for 25 to 35 minutes, or until the chicken is cooked through. (The time will depend on the size of the breast: they will be 180°F at the thickest part.) Serve hot from the oven, drizzled with a little more olive oil.

ASIAN CHICKEN LETTUCE WRAPS

When I can't think of what to serve my family for dinner, I know these lettuce wraps will always be well received. My kids love them because they can make their own. I love them because they are so easy and fast. We all love the flavor and crunch of the lettuce against the cooked chicken.

Serves 4

4 tablespoons sesame or olive oil

1 pound ground chicken

Kosher salt and freshly ground black pepper

2 garlic cloves, peeled and finely minced

1 (1-inch) piece ginger, peeled and finely minced

½ red bell pepper, finely diced

4 ounces water chestnuts, drained

½ cup soy sauce

3 tablespoons hoisin sauce

4 scallions, trimmed and sliced

12 whole Bibb lettuce leaves

Sprigs of cilantro and fresh mint, for garnish

In a large sauté pan, heat 2 tablespoons of the oil until shimmering over medium-high heat and cook the ground chicken, breaking it up with a wooden spoon, until cooked through. Season with salt and pepper and transfer to a bowl.

Add the remaining 2 tablespoons of the oil in the sauté pan over medium heat and when hot, cook the garlic and ginger for about 1 minute, stirring to prevent burning. Add the pepper and cook for 1 to 2 minutes longer or until the pepper softens. Return the chicken to the pan and stir in the chestnuts to mix all the ingredients.

In a small cup, whisk the soy sauce and hoisin with ¼ cup of water. Pour into the pan, add the scallions, and simmer for 1 minute, stirring to mix.

Remove the chicken from the heat and spoon the mixture into the Bibb lettuce leaves, which should cup the chicken. Garnish with sprigs of cilantro and mint, as desired.

PAN-ROASTED DUCK WITH CHERRY SAUCE

Duck is so succulent and tasty, I couldn't resist including it here. This dish is easy to prepare, yet swanky enough for a dinner party. And there is no need to roast a whole duck; buy duck breasts, which are getting easier to find in supermarkets and are the tastiest part of the duck. While the USDA recommends cooking duck to an internal temperature of 170°F, I like to cook it until its internal temperature is 135° to 140° F, at which point the meat is medium-rare. Ducks naturally have a lot of fat and so instead of discarding the rendered fat, save it to sauté potatoes and vegetables. Unbelievable! If you have dried cherries on hand, you can substitute them for the fresh. Your choice.

Serves 4

4 (10-ounce) duck breasts

Kosher salt and freshly ground black pepper

¼ cup finely diced shallots

1 teaspoon chopped fresh thyme

1 cup Port

3 tablespoons balsamic vinegar

½ cup pitted fresh cherries

1 tablespoon honey

2 tablespoons cold unsalted butter

Pat the duck breasts dry with a paper towel; they will be damp when removed from the package. With a small, sharp knife, cut four diagonal slashes, about ¼-inch deep, on the fat side of each breast. Repeat the process in the other direction for a crosshatch design. Season the duck generously with salt and pepper.

Meanwhile, heat a large sauté pan over medium heat.

Put the breasts, fat side down, in the pan and cook for about 15 minutes until the fat has rendered and the breasts are deep, golden brown. Turn the breasts over and cook for about 6 minutes longer, or until medium-rare and the meat registers 135° to 140°F on an instant-read thermometer. For a greater degree of doneness, let it cook until the thermometer registers 165° to 170°F. Remove from the pan and let the duck breasts rest while you prepare the sauce.

Pour off all but 1 teaspoon of fat from the pan. (Save the excess fat for cooking potatoes.) Add the shallots and cook, stirring constantly, for 1 to 2 minutes over medium heat. Add the thyme, cook for a few seconds, and then add the Port, balsamic vinegar, cherries, and honey, raise the heat, and bring to a boil. Boil the sauce for 4 to 5 minutes or until the sauce begins to reduce and thicken. Swirl in the butter, a tablespoon at a time, and season the sauce with salt and pepper.

Put the duck breasts on each of four plates and spoon the sauce over the duck. Serve right away.

CHAPTER 4

LET'S GRILL TONIGHT

IN PARTS OF THE COUNTRY WITH COLD
WEATHER FOUR OR FIVE MONTHS OUT OF
THE YEAR, GRILLING IS SEASONAL. In other regions,
the outdoor grill is pretty much an extension of the kitchen. As Americans have
become increasingly enamored of cooking outside, we've invested in easy-to-use
gas grills, some fitted with any number of elaborate features such as rotisseries and
side burners. Other backyard grill masters are die-hard fans of charcoal, eschewing
food cooked on gas. Some of us swing back and forth between gas and charcoal,
as the spirit, the weather, our time constraints, and the recipe dictate.

I live in the Northeast and so am constrained by weather. Still, I tend to use
the grill a lot during the summer and well into the fall. Meals cooked in the open
are always a little more fun and the food tastes extra good. Some of the recipes
included in this chapter call for marinating, but not all. Marinades add good flavor
and are fun to create. They also encourage preparing ahead, which always makes
it easier to get the meal on the table. The marinades, chutneys, and other accompaniments that are specified for one recipe usually can be transferred to another
where the meat, fish or chicken is simply grilled and calling out for some extra zing.
You can't go wrong.

GRILLED RIB EYE STEAKS WITH ROSEMARY CHIMICHURRI

This is grilling at its most elementary and, some would argue, its best. Slap a few big, juicy steaks on the grill and anticipate an awesome meal to come. A lot of people serve bottled steak sauce with grilled steak but I prefer a heady, herbaceous South American concoction. The Argentines love their meat, particularly beef, and most often grill it over hot fires. These people know a thing or two about what best complements perfectly cooked steak: an intense, garlicky herb sauce called chimichurri, always made with lots of parsley. I have added some pungent rosemary to the mix for an especially aromatic garnish.

Serves 4

4 (16-ounce) bone-in rib eye steaks, about 1 1/4-inches thick

Kosher salt and freshly ground black pepper

Rosemary Chimichurri (recipe follows on page 104)

Spray the grilling grate of a gas or charcoal grill with vegetable oil spray. Preheat the grill to medium hot.

Season the steaks generously with salt and pepper. Grill for about 5 minutes on each side for medium-rare meat. Increase the cooking time for better done steak.

Let the steak rest for about 5 minutes before serving with the chimichurri.

ROSEMARY CHIMICHURRI

Makes about 1 cup

2 cups packed flat-leaf parsley leaves

½ cup fresh rosemary leaves

½ cup extra-virgin olive oil

4 whole garlic cloves

2 tablespoons fresh lemon juice

1 teaspoon kosher salt

¼ teaspoon dried red pepper flakes

In the bowl of a food processor, blend the parsley, rosemary, olive oil, garlic, lemon juice, salt, and red pepper flakes until smooth. Use right away or cover and refrigerate for up to a week.

CHIPOTLE, LIME, AND HONEY GRILLED FLANK STEAK

During the summer we cater a lot of outdoor parties at Aux Délices and this flank steak recipe is one of our most popular. The combination of fierce chipotle peppers, lime juice, garlic, and cilantro blends perfectly with the touch of honey and Worcestershire. It's never overpowering but makes a tasty statement. Once a can of chipotle peppers in adobo sauce is opened, the best way to save the contents is to divide small amounts of peppers and sauce between plastic bags or ice cube trays and freeze to use in later recipes.

Serves 4 to 6

3 tablespoons Worcestershire sauce

2 tablespoons honey

¼ cup canola oil

Grated zest and juice of 3 limes

½ cup chopped cilantro

4 garlic cloves, thinly sliced

3 chipotle peppers in adobo sauce, plus 3 tablespoons adobo sauce

1½ to 2 pounds flank steak

Mix together the Worcestershire sauce, honey, canola oil, and lime juice. Add the cilantro, garlic, peppers, adobo sauce, and the lime zest. Use a whisk to break the peppers into small pieces.

Lay the steak in a glass, ceramic, or other nonreactive dish. Pour the marinade over the steak and turn the steak a few times to coat well. Cover with plastic wrap and refrigerate for at least 8 hours and up to 12 hours or overnight. Turn the steak once or twice during marinating.

Spray the grilling grate of a gas or charcoal grill with vegetable oil spray. Preheat the grill to medium hot.

Lift the steak from the marinade and wipe the excess from the meat. Grill the meat for 4 to 5 minutes on each side for medium-rare, or until done to your liking.

Let the meat rest for about 10 minutes before slicing across the grain and serving.

GRILLED LEG OF LAMB WITH MUSTARD AND GARLIC

If you like leg of lamb, you'll love this simple, straightforward way of grilling it, boned and flattened— also called butterflied—so that it cooks relatively quickly over good, hot coals. It's far easier than roasting a bone-in lamb in the oven. I decided on a classic marinade made from mustard, red wine, and garlic, as well as some generous handfuls of fresh herbs. The time the lamb soaks in this savory brew heightens its flavors so that all you need to do is watch the meat for about half an hour as it grills. It's important to take the meat from the fridge about an hour before cooking; cold meat does not cook as evenly as does room-temperature meat. I like the lamb just as it is when it comes off the grill, but the mint-flavored mustard is wonderful with it, too.

Serves 8

10 garlic cloves

¼ cup chopped fresh rosemary

¼ cup chopped fresh mint

1 (5- to 6-pound) butterflied leg of lamb

¾ cup Dijon mustard

¾ cup red wine

½ cup canola oil

2 tablespoons herbes de Provence

Kosher salt and freshly ground black pepper

Minted-Honey Mustard (recipe follows)

Cut four of the garlic cloves in half. Roughly chop the remaining six.

Mix together the rosemary and mint.

Spread the lamb open on a flat work surface. Using the tip of a small, sharp knife, make eight small slits into the meat on the inside of the lamb. Stuff the halved garlic cloves into the slits. Spread the mixed herbs over both sides of the lamb. Transfer the lamb to a glass, ceramic, or other nonreactive dish large enough to hold it opened up.

Mix together the mustard, wine, oil, herbes de Provence, and the remaining garlic. Pour over the lamb, cover the dish, and refrigerate the lamb for at least 8 hours or overnight.

Remove the lamb from the refrigerator about 1 hour before grilling. Wipe off the marinade and remove and discard the garlic halves. Lay the lamb on a clean platter and season both sides with salt and pepper.

Spray the grilling grate of a gas or charcoal grill with vegetable oil spray. Preheat the grill to medium hot.

Grill the lamb for 12 to 15 minutes on each side for medium-rare lamb: The internal temperature will read 145°F for medium-rare. The exact time will depend on the thickness of the butterflied leg of lamb and the desired degree of doneness.

Let the lamb rest on a cutting board for 10 to 15 minutes before slicing against the grain. Serve with the Minted-Honey Mustard.

MINTED-HONEY MUSTARD

Makes about ¹/₂ cup

¹/₃ cup Dijon mustard

2 to 3 tablespoons honey, or as needed

1 tablespoon white balsamic vinegar

1 teaspoon chopped rosemary

1 tablespoon chopped mint leaves

Stir together the mustard, honey, vinegar, rosemary, and mint. Taste and add more honey if desired.

The mustard can be made up to 24 hours ahead of time. Let the mustard reach room temperature before serving.

YOGURT AND SPICE GRILLED FLANK STEAK

Vermillion, a restaurant near Grand Central Station in New York City, serves flank steak with a yogurt–sour cream marinade that is really delicious. I came up with my own version and am pleased as punch with the outcome. The spices mixed with the tartness of the sour cream and yogurt blend perfectly with rich flank or skirt steak. Whenever you grill steak, it's important to watch it carefully so that it does not overcook. You can always put it back on the grill if it's too rare but you can't retrieve its juiciness if it's overdone.

Serves 4 to 6

1 cup sour cream

³/₄ cup plain yogurt

2 teaspoons ground cumin

2 teaspoons ground curry powder

4 garlic cloves, thinly sliced

¹/₂ small jalapeño pepper, seeded and thinly sliced

2 pounds flank or skirt steak

Mix together the sour cream, yogurt, cumin, curry powder, garlic, and jalapeño.

Lay the steak in a glass, ceramic, or other nonreactive dish. Pour the marinade over the steak and turn the steak a few times to coat well. Cover with plastic wrap and refrigerate for 6 to 8 hours or overnight. Turn the steak once or twice during marinating.

Spray the grilling grate of a gas or charcoal grill with vegetable oil spray. Preheat the grill to medium hot.

Lift the steak from the marinade and wipe the excess from the meat. Grill the meat for 4 to 5 minutes on each side for medium-rare, or until done to your liking.

Let the meat rest for about 10 minutes before slicing across the grain and serving. (See page 109 for more.)

Flank Steak on the Grill

Flank steak is one of my very favorite cuts of beef. It's leaner than some others but has amazing flavor and a fantastically pleasing coarse texture that is hard to find in other steaks. Sometimes called London broil, it's a flat-ish piece of meat that can be stuffed and rolled, although most of the time I grill flank steak flat out (the best way, if you ask me).

If you can't find flank steak or want to try something a little difference, try skirt or hanger steak. These two cuts are close to flank in terms of flavor and texture. Skirt steak is a long, flat cut with more flavor than tenderness. The same goes for hanger steak, which has gotten a lot attention in recent years. The ungainly steak is also called butcher's steak because, the story goes, the double-lobed steak connected by a particularly tough sinew was prized by butchers for its flavor even though its homely appearance made it tough to sell. While hangers are delicious when cooked right, I prefer skirt steak as a stand-in for flank steak.

All recipes for flank steak instruct you to "slice the meat across the grain." If that directive baffles you, consider that the meat is made up of long, relatively tough fibers that must be intersected with a knife to shorten them and make the meat tender enough to chew easily. You can see these fibers in the meat. To cut a flank steak correctly all you must to do is slice it on the bias, the diagonal, across those long fibers.

SUPERSTAR TERIYAKI SALMON

Grilled salmon is always a winner, even if simply brushed with olive oil and seasoned with salt and pepper before cooking. But if you decide to marinate the fish in a teriyaki sauce, it's a superstar. I love teriyaki in general for salmon, chicken, and beef. It can be adjusted so easily to suit your taste by adding more or less garlic, ginger, and sugar. Toss in some grated orange zest to perk up the flavors. If you cook the marinade gently over a low flame, it will turn thick and syrupy, a perfect glaze for salmon, tuna, or just about any kind of firm-fleshed fish. When I use it to marinate the salmon for just a few hours—if I am pressed for time—I omit the water to concentrate the flavors.

Serves 4

½ cup soy sauce

3 tablespoons brown sugar or honey

2 tablespoons peeled and minced ginger

2 garlic cloves, sliced

4 scallions, trimmed and sliced, white and light green parts

4 salmon fillets (each about 5 ounces)

Kosher salt and freshly ground black pepper

Mix together the soy sauce, brown sugar, ginger, garlic, and scallions, add ⅓ cup of water, and bring to a boil in a small saucepan over medium-high heat. Reduce the heat to medium and simmer for about 2 minutes, until reduced and syrupy. Let the teriyaki sauce cool.

Lay the salmon fillets in a glass, ceramic, or other nonreactive container large enough to hold them in a single layer. Pour the teriyaki sauce over them, cover, and refrigerate for at least 6 hours and up to 12 hours, or overnight. Turn the salmon once or twice during marinating.

Spray the grilling grate of a gas or charcoal grill with vegetable oil spray. Heat the grill so that the heating elements or coals are medium hot.

Lift the salmon from the marinade, let the excess drip from the fillets, and then season them with salt and pepper. Grill the fish for 3 to 4 minutes on each side, depending on the thickness of the fillets. Serve immediately.

CHICKEN TIKI KEBABS

These chicken skewers cook quickly on the grill; watch them carefully but don't move them around too much at first so they don't stick to the grill. After the chicken has soaked for hours in the highly seasoned yogurt, it's exceptionally flavorful and moist—perfect with a green salad, some rice, or maybe just good, crusty bread. I particularly like this because it has such a long and forgiving lead time, making it easy to make well ahead of time.

Serves 4

1 cup plain Greek yogurt

¼ cup chopped cilantro

3 garlic cloves, minced

1 teaspoon ground cumin

1 teaspoon kosher salt, plus more for seasoning

½ teaspoon curry powder

¼ teaspoon chili powder

Freshly ground black pepper

1½ pounds boneless, skinless chicken breast halves, cut into 1-inch chunks

Mix together the yogurt, cilantro, garlic, cumin, salt, curry powder, and chili. Season to taste with pepper. Add the chicken pieces, stir to mix well, cover, and refrigerate for at 6 to 8 hours or overnight.

Lift the chicken from the marinade, wipe off the excess, and thread the chicken onto metal skewers.

Spray the grilling grate of a gas or charcoal grill with vegetable oil spray. Heat the grill so that the heating elements or coals are medium hot.

Season the kebabs with salt and pepper and grill for about 4 minutes per side, or until cooked through. Serve immediately.

GRILLED CURRIED SHRIMP

This simple marinade works beautifully with shrimp, but I have also bathed chicken in it. I like the grilled shrimp without the salsa, but it's even better with it, adding a cool crunch.

Serves 4 ⊗⊙⊗⊙⊗⊙⊗⊙⊗⊙⊗⊙⊗⊙⊗⊙⊗⊙⊗⊙⊗⊙⊗⊙⊗⊙⊗⊙⊗⊙⊗⊙⊗⊙⊗

1 tablespoon, plus 1 teaspoon curry powder

²/₃ cup canola oil

Grated zest of 2 lemons

2 tablespoons chopped cilantro leaves

24 large shrimp, peeled and cleaned (about 1¼ pounds)

Juice of ½ lemon

Kosher salt and freshly ground black pepper

Pineapple-Jicama Salsa (recipe follows on page 114)

Stir together the curry powder, oil, lemon zest, and cilantro and toss the shrimp in the marinade to coat. Refrigerate, covered, for at least 6 hours and up to 12 hours or overnight.

Spray the grilling grate of a gas or charcoal grill with vegetable oil spray. Preheat the grill to medium hot.

Lift the shrimp from the marinade and arrange on a clean plate. Squeeze the lemon over the shrimp. Thread the shrimp on four metal skewers, six shrimp on each skewer with a little space between each one. Season with salt and pepper.

Grill the shrimp for 2 to 3 minutes on each side until cooked through. Serve with the pineapple salsa.

PINEAPPLE-JICAMA SALSA

Makes about 1 1/2 cups ⋙⋙⋙⋙⋙⋙⋙⋙⋙⋙⋙⋙⋙⋙

1 cup diced pineapple

½ cup diced jicama

2 tablespoons finely chopped cilantro leaves

2 tablespoons finely diced red onion

2 tablespoons olive oil

2 tablespoons finely diced jalapeño pepper

Juice of 1 lime

Kosher salt and freshly ground black pepper

Stir together the pineapple, jicama, cilantro, red onion, olive oil, jalapeño, and lime juice. Season to taste with salt and pepper and serve.

The salsa can be made up to 24 hours ahead of time. Let the salsa come to room temperature before serving.

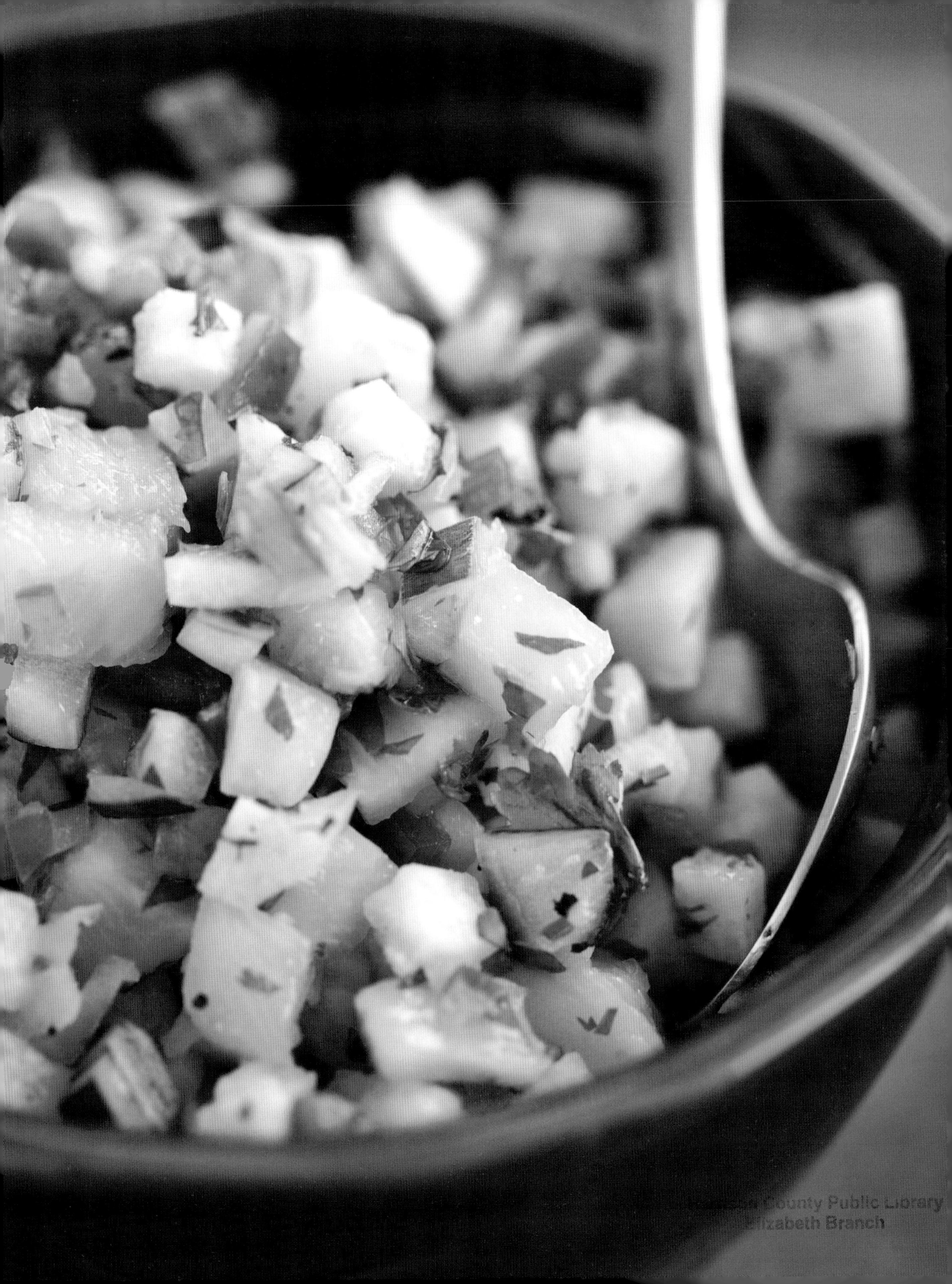

BUTTERMILK GRILLED CHICKEN

On one of my appearances on the Today Show, I was asked for an easy summer grilling recipe and decided to make this. The buttermilk and spices are wonderful with the chicken, which can soak in the marinade for hours before grilling. It tastes great, is more healthful, and is far easier to cook than more traditional buttermilk fried chicken. I especially like to marinate chicken in buttermilk because it activates the enzymes in the meat that break down the proteins and contribute to its tenderness.

Serves 6 to 8

3 cups buttermilk

6 garlic cloves, thinly sliced

1 tablespoon cumin

1 tablespoon chili powder

2 teaspoons kosher salt, plus more for seasoning

1 teaspoon ground coriander

1 teaspoon smoked or regular paprika

3 ½ to 4 pounds assorted chicken pieces, such as halved breasts, legs, thighs

Freshly ground black pepper

Mix together the buttermilk, garlic, cumin, chili powder, 2 teaspoons of salt, coriander, and paprika. Lay the chicken pieces in a single layer in a glass, ceramic, or other nonreactive baking dish. Pour the marinade over the chicken, making sure every piece is covered. Cover with plastic wrap and refrigerate for at least 8 hours or up to 12 hours or overnight.

Spray the grilling grate of a gas or charcoal grill with vegetable oil spray. Preheat the grill to medium hot.

Drain the marinade from the chicken and pat the chicken pieces with paper towels to dry them. Season them with salt and pepper and grill for 12 to 15 minutes until cooked through, turning the chicken pieces once or twice during grilling. The time will vary depending on the size of the piece. Serve right away or at warm room temperature.

How to Keep Chicken Moist on the Grill

The best way I have found to prevent chicken breasts from drying out on the grill or for any quick-cooking method is to brine the chicken for up to 45 minutes. This works particularly well for boneless, skinless chicken breasts—the go-to cuts for easy, quick cooking. Because they are skinless, they tend to dry out quickly. Once they are brined, they can be used in the recipe.

Brines are not difficult to make. As the word suggests, they are nothing more than salted water, usually with some other seasonings. Here is the brine I make for soaking up to six boneless, skinless chicken breasts. Once they are brined, lift the breasts from the liquid, pat them dry, and get cooking.

QUICK BRINE FOR CHICKEN

Makes about 8 cups

8 cups cold water

¼ cup kosher salt

¼ cup sugar

Bring 1 ½ to 2 cups of the cold water to a boil. Remove the pot from the heat and stir in the salt and sugar until dissolved. Add the rest of the water. Cool the brine completely.

Submerge the chicken in the brine and refrigerate for 30 to 45 minutes. Pat the chicken breast dry, season lightly with salt and pepper, and then grill or pan-fry according to the recipe. At this time, you can season and cook the chicken according to a recipe.

NOTE: I often jazz up the brine by adding crushed peppercorns or coriander seeds, cayenne, fennel seeds, orange or lemon slices and peel to the hot water along with the salt and sugar.

GRILLED CHICKEN PAILLARD WITH NECTARINE CHUTNEY

The crowning glory of this very simple recipe for grilled chicken is the chutney, which marries nectarines with summer's best tomatoes, a partnership with no equal. The chutney can be made ahead of time, and the chicken takes minutes to grill—so this could easily be a fast, simple dinner on a summer night. Also think about making a sandwich with the cold grilled chicken, accented with the chutney.

Serves 4

4 boneless skinless chicken breasts

Kosher salt and freshly ground black pepper

2 tablespoons extra-virgin olive oil

Nectarine Chutney (recipe follows)

Lay each chicken breast between two sheets of plastic wrap and pound with a meat mallet or the flat side of a small, heavy skillet until $1/4$-inch thick. Season the paillards with salt and pepper.

Spray the grilling grate of a gas or charcoal grill with vegetable oil spray. Preheat the grill to medium hot.

Grill the chicken for 2 to 3 minutes on each side or until cooked through.

Lift the chicken from the grill and brush each paillard with olive oil. Serve the chicken immediately with Nectarine Chutney spooned on top.

NECTARINE CHUTNEY

Makes about 2 cups

1 tablespoon olive oil

1 shallot, finely diced

1 garlic clove, minced

1¼ teaspoons curry powder

2 ripe nectarines (about 1 pound), pitted and cut into medium dice

1 small ripe tomato, diced

3 tablespoons brown sugar

2 tablespoons apple cider vinegar

Salt and freshly ground black pepper

In a medium saucepan, heat the oil over medium heat and when hot, cook the shallot and garlic, stirring, for about 1 minute. Take care the garlic does not burn. Stir in the curry powder and cook for a few seconds.

Add the nectarines, tomato, brown sugar, and vinegar and bring to a simmer. Cover the pan and cook for about 10 minutes, stirring occasionally and breaking up the nectarines and tomatoes as it is stirred. Raise the heat to medium-high and cook, uncovered, for 5 to 6 minutes longer or until thick and syrupy. Season to taste with salt and pepper. Serve the chutney warm or at room temperature.

SOY AND SAKE GRILLED TUNA

The vegetables, liberally dressed with sesame vinaigrette, add crunch and freshness to the grilled tuna. Before it's dressed with the veggies and before it's grilled, the tuna swims in a simple, Japanese-inspired marinade, which is equally delicious with salmon.

Serves 4

¾ cup soy sauce

½ cup sake

4 scallions, trimmed and thinly sliced

4 garlic cloves, thinly sliced

2 tablespoons mirin or sweet sherry

Juice and grated zest of 1 lime

4 (5- to 6-ounce) pieces high-quality tuna, each about ¾-inch thick

Kosher salt and freshly ground black pepper

Vegetables in Sesame Vinaigrette (recipe follows)

In a large glass, ceramic, or other nonreactive dish, mix together the soy sauce, sake, scallions, garlic, mirin, and lime juice and zest. Add the tuna, turn to coat, cover and refrigerate for at least 3 hours and up to 6 hours. Turn once during marinating.

Spray the grilling grate of a gas or charcoal grill with vegetable oil spray. Heat the grill so that the heating elements or coals are medium hot.

Lift the tuna from the marinade and season on both sides with salt and pepper. Grill the tuna for about 2 minutes on each side, which keeps it rare to medium-rare in the center.

Put a piece of tuna on each of four serving plates and top with a few spoonfuls of the vegetables. Serve right away.

VEGETABLES IN SESAME VINAIGRETTE

Makes about ³/₄ cup

1 teaspoon sesame seeds

3 tablespoons rice wine vinegar or white wine vinegar

¼ teaspoon kosher salt

¼ cup sesame oil

1 small red bell pepper, seeded and thinly sliced

2 scallions, trimmed and thinly sliced

¼ small red onion, very thinly sliced

In a small dry pan, spread the sesame seeds in a layer and cook over medium heat for about 1 minute, or until they turn golden brown and are fragrant. Remove from the heat and set aside to cool.

Whisk together the vinegar and salt until the salt dissolves. Still whisking, slowly drizzle in the oil until incorporated. Add the pepper slices, scallions, and red onions and toss to mix. Sprinkle the sesame seeds over the vegetables and serve.

If not using right away, cover and refrigerate. Stir well before using.

CHAPTER 5

ON THE SLOW SIDE

SOMETIMES THE BEST MEAL IS THE ONE THAT TAKES THE LONGEST TO COOK. I don't mean the longest to prepare: I am referring to cooking time. While it's a bonus that most of the work is done by the heat of the oven or stovetop, the real reward is that these dishes always hit the spot. Take the short ribs (admittedly my idea of a blue ribbon braise). They are fall-off-the-bone tender, full of flavor, and so, so comforting on a windy, stormy day. And if you are lucky enough to have leftovers, the meat, pulled from the bones, can be mixed with fresh pappardelle or rigatoni the next day for one of the best pasta dishes going.

For the most part, the recipes in this chapter are easy to put together and then are transferred to the oven or left to cook on the stovetop while you go about your life. Meanwhile, the kitchen fills with gorgeous aromas that waft about the house, welcoming everyone who walks through the door and prompting those familiar words: "When's dinner?"

Some of these recipes don't take hours to cook but instead taste as though they did. I am thinking of the chili recipes in particular, which cook fairly quickly. The turkey chili is one of our top sellers at Aux Délices, a much-loved family favorite that is more healthful than other chilies. Like stews and braises, these dishes taste just as good or even better the day after they are cooked.

So, give yourself a break. Try the risotto, which cooks in the oven. No stirring required. Make this the year you make beef stew or pot roast (you will be asked to make it again and again once your family gets a taste). Best of all: slow down!

PUMPKIN CHILI

This one took a while to get right but I am as happy with this chili as a kid with a bulging bag of Halloween candy. When I say "pumpkin chili," the expression on people's faces is priceless because it sounds like an oddity—and yet it's easy, healthful, and so delicious. A couple of years ago, my family and some friends went to a pumpkin festival in Pennsylvania Amish country. While we tried pumpkin bowling and football, we also ate all manner of foods made with pumpkin. Cold and hungry, we dug into some pumpkin chili and my taste memory is that it was about the best thing I had ever put in my mouth. It took a few tries to get the flavors really right but finally success was mine! Hope your family likes it as much as mine does.

Serves 6

4 tablespoons canola oil

1 pound lean ground beef

Kosher salt and freshly ground black pepper

1 medium onion, diced

1 green bell pepper, seeded and diced

3 garlic cloves, peeled and thinly sliced

1 zucchini, diced

1 cup peeled and diced butternut squash

1 (15-ounce) can plain, unseasoned pumpkin purée

2 cups canned crushed plum tomatoes and juices

(continued)

Heat 2 tablespoons of the oil over medium-high heat in a large sauté pan until shimmering. Cook the beef, breaking it up with a wooden spoon, until browned and cooked through and it is in small pieces. Add about 1 1/2 teaspoons of salt and season to taste with pepper. Drain the meat and set aside.

In the same pan, heat the remaining 2 tablespoons of oil over medium-high heat (if you use the same pan, wipe it clean). When hot, cook the onion, green pepper, and garlic for 5 to 6 minutes or until the vegetables are tender.

Return the meat to the pan along with the zucchini, squash, pumpkin purée, tomatoes, stock, pumpkin pie spice, cumin, chili powder, and about 1 1/2 teaspoons of salt. Bring to a boil, reduce the heat, cover, and cook at a gentle simmer for about 30 minutes or until the butternut squash is tender. Adjust the heat to maintain the simmer.

Add the kidney beans, stir the chili well, heat through, and serve.

2 cups chicken stock, preferably homemade

1 teaspoon pumpkin pie spice

1 teaspoon cumin

$^3/_4$ teaspoon chili powder

1 (15-ounce) can kidney beans, drained and rinsed

TURKEY CHILI

I would never have used canned kidney beans years ago, when I thought it was somehow "cheating." In those days, I was more of a purist. No more. These days I am just as apt to open a couple of cans as to start with dried beans. I do still start with dried beans when I have the time because I like their texture but using canned beans makes this easy to serve on weeknights. It's not really slow cooking, but I think it belongs in this chapter because it tastes as though it simmered for hours: thick, hearty and good for you!

Serves 6 to 8

3 tablespoons olive oil

1 pound ground turkey, preferably dark meat

1 medium onion, cut into small dice

2 garlic cloves, minced

¾ teaspoon chili powder

1 teaspoon ground cumin

¼ teaspoon cayenne pepper

Kosher salt and freshly ground black pepper

1 (28-ounce) can crushed tomatoes

2 (15-ounce) cans kidney beans

½ cup sour cream

½ red onion, finely diced

1 cup grated Cheddar cheese (about 3 ounces)

Heat 1 tablespoon of the oil over medium-high heat in a large sauté pan until shimmering. Cook the ground turkey, stirring it with a wooden spoon to break it up, until cooked through. Tip the turkey and any oil into a colander and let it drain.

Add the remaining 2 tablespoons of oil to the pan and when hot, cook the onion, garlic, chili powder, cumin, cayenne, and 1 teaspoon of salt, stirring occasionally, for 4 to 5 minutes or until the onions are softened and lightly colored. Season to taste with pepper.

Add the tomatoes, 2 cups water, and turkey and cook over medium-low heat for about 20 minutes, stirring occasionally. Add the beans and cook for 10 minutes longer. Season with salt and pepper to taste and cook until the chili is heated through and the flavors are balanced. Add more chili powder if needed, according to your personal taste.

Serve garnished with sour cream, chopped onion, and grated cheese.

APPLE CIDER PORK CHOPS

It's so easy to get the pork chops in a marinade first thing in the morning. Then, they'll be ready to cook at the end of the day. The marinade makes a fantastic sauce for the meat, pulling everything together for a perfect fall meal. I put this with the other "slow" recipes because of the long marinating time.

Serves 4

1 cup apple cider

½ cup packed dark brown sugar

½ cup maple syrup

⅓ cup Dijon mustard

4 boneless pork chops, each 1-inch thick

Kosher salt and freshly ground black pepper

2 tablespoons canola oil

Mix together the cider, brown sugar, maple syrup, and mustard.

Put the pork chops in a glass, ceramic, or other nonreactive dish just big enough to hold them snugly in a single layer. Pour the cider marinade over the chops, turn them to coat evenly, and then cover with plastic wrap. Refrigerate for at least 6 hours and up to 12 hours or overnight. Longer is better. Turn the chops over once during marinating.

Lift the pork chops from the marinade and let any excess marinade drip back into the dish. Season the chops lightly with salt and pepper.

Heat the oil in a large sauté pan over medium-high heat. When hot, cook the pork chops for about 8 minutes on each side or until cooked through. An instant-read thermometer inserted in the thickest part of the chops will register 150°F. Transfer the pork chops to serving plates.

Meanwhile, pour the marinade into a saucepan and bring to a boil over high heat. Reduce the heat to medium and cook for 10 to 12 minutes or until thick and syrupy. Serve the reduced sauce with the pork chops.

BAKED WILD MUSHROOM RISOTTO

While this wonderful risotto can be dressed up for a dinner party, it's also a great family meal made as described here. To fancy it up, add some cooked lobster, asparagus, and a drizzle of truffle oil. One of the best things about it is that you don't have to spend a lot of time stirring the pot!

Serves 6

2 tablespoons olive oil

3 whole garlic cloves

1 small Spanish onion, finely diced

8 ounces mixed wild mushrooms, such as cremini, shiitake, and oyster, sliced or halved, if necessary, depending on the size of the mushrooms

4 cups chicken or vegetable stock, preferably homemade

1½ cups Arborio rice

4 ounces mascarpone cheese

½ cup grated Parmesan cheese

1 tablespoon unsalted butter

2 teaspoons kosher salt

Freshly ground black pepper

Preheat the oven to 350°F.

In a Dutch oven or similar pot with a tight-fitting lid, heat the olive oil over medium heat and when shimmering, sauté the garlic and onion for 3 to 4 minutes or until softened. Add the mushrooms and sauté for about 2 minutes or until golden brown.

Bring the stock to a boil and pour into the pot with the mushrooms. Stir in the rice, cover, and transfer to the oven for about 40 minutes, or until most of the stock is absorbed and the rice is creamy.

Remove from the oven and stir in the mascarpone and Parmesan cheese and the butter until melted. Season with salt and pepper and serve immediately.

SUNDAY POT ROAST

Pot roast is synonymous with long, slow cooking and just happens to be one of my all-time favorites, especially in frigid or inclement weather when a little comfort food is called for. The glory of this is that the oven does most of the work, and when I have the foresight to make this a day ahead of time, it tastes even better.

Serves 4 to 6

3 ½ pounds boneless beef chuck roast

Kosher salt and freshly ground black pepper

2 tablespoons canola oil

3 cups beef stock

1 cup red wine

2 tablespoons tomato paste

4 garlic cloves, peeled and sliced

2 sprigs fresh rosemary

4 carrots, peeled and cut into large dice

4 parsnips, peeled and cut into large dice

1 large white onion, cut into large dice

1 large potato, peeled and cut into large dice

(continued)

Preheat oven to 325°F.

Generously season the meat with salt and pepper. Heat the canola oil over medium-high heat in a Dutch oven or similar pot with a tight-fitting lid until just smoking. Sear the meat for about 10 minutes, turning to brown lightly on all sides. Add the stock, wine, tomato paste, garlic, and rosemary. The liquid should reach halfway up the meat and if it does not, add a little more stock or water.

Cover the Dutch oven, put it in the center of the oven, and roast for 2 hours, turning the meat halfway through cooking.

After 2 hours of cooking, add the carrots, parsnips, onion, and potato, stir to mix, cover the Dutch oven, and return it to the oven for about 1 ½ hours longer, or until the meat is fork-tender and cooked through.

Lift the meat from the pot and transfer to a platter or large plate and cover loosely with aluminum foil to keep warm. Using a slotted spoon, transfer the vegetables to a bowl and cover to keep warm.

2 tablespoons all-purpose
flour

2 tablespoons unsalted
butter, melted (if needed)

2 teaspoons fresh thyme
leaves

1 to 2 tablespoons chopped
flat-leaf parsley

Skim off any fat from the surface of the liquid. Put the skimmed fat in a small saucepan, add the flour, and whisk over low heat until smooth and pastelike. If there is not enough fat to accomplish this, add the melted butter to the pan. Spoon two or three ladles of the cooking broth into the pan and whisk to mix with the flour paste. Raise the heat and bring to a boil. As soon as the sauce boils, pour it into the Dutch oven. Return the sauce to a boil over medium-high heat, reduce the heat to medium, and simmer for about 5 minutes, or until the gravy thickens.

Remove the rosemary leaves from the stems, if you can, and return the leaves to the Dutch oven with the thyme. Season to taste with salt and pepper.

Slice the pot roast and serve it with the vegetables and thickened gravy, garnished with parsley.

BRAISED SHORT RIBS

I love short ribs more than any other braised meat. If you haven't tried them at home, may I suggest you wait no longer? When I make these on a lazy weekend afternoon, I happily anticipate the full-flavored, fall-off-the-bone meat to come: my absolute favorite. The prep is not difficult and then the ribs and veggies spend a long time in the oven while I sit by the fire (or do the laundry is more like it). This is as good served over egg noodles as with the polenta on page 217.

Serves 4

2 tablespoons canola oil

4 pounds bone-in beef short ribs

Salt and freshly ground black pepper

4 ribs celery, cut into 1-inch-long pieces

2 carrots, cut into 1-inch-long pieces

2 onions, cut into large dice

6 whole garlic cloves

2 tablespoons all-purpose flour

2 tablespoons tomato paste

2 cups red wine

2 cups beef stock, preferably homemade

(continued)

Preheat the oven to 350°F. Arrange the oven racks so that one is right in the center and there will be enough room for a Dutch oven.

Heat the oil in a large Dutch oven or similar pot over high heat.

Season the short ribs with salt and pepper and sear them, turning several times until browned on all sides. You will have to do this in batches; do not crowd the pot. Transfer the ribs to a plate when they are browned.

Add the celery, carrots, onions, and garlic to the pot and cook over medium-high heat, stirring often. Take care not to let the garlic burn. Add the flour and tomato paste and cook for 1 to 2 minutes longer, stirring constantly.

Add the wine and stock, scraping the bottom of the pot with a wooden spoon to scrape up any browned particles. Bring to a boil and then return the ribs to the pot. Add the thyme, bay leaves, oregano, and rosemary, cover, and transfer to the center rack of the oven.

Braise for about 2 1/2 hours or until meat is very tender and easily separates from the bone. Remove the meat and bones from the pot and arrange on a serving platter.

6 sprigs fresh thyme

2 bay leaves

2 sprigs fresh oregano

1 sprig fresh rosemary

¼ cup chopped flat-leaf parsley

Strain the sauce through a colander or large sieve into a large saucepan or bowl, pressing on the vegetables to extract as much liquid as possible. Bring to a boil over medium-high heat, skimming off any fat that accumulates on the surface. Reduce the heat to medium and cook for about 15 minutes or until the sauce is slightly thickened and its flavors intensify. Season to taste with salt and pepper.

Pour the sauce over the ribs, garnish with chopped parsley, and serve.

A Pinch of Salt

I use kosher salt throughout the book, but you could just as easily use sea salt, if that's your preference and what you have in your cupboard. I like the way kosher salt feels and seasons food, and because of its relatively large crystals, I can tell how much I am holding between my fingers.

I don't recommend table salt, however, as I rarely use it. It is mined from underground caves and I find its sharp, mineral-y saltiness distracting. In the early days of the twentieth century, salt manufacturers added iodine to table salt to combat iodine deficiencies in much of the population. We no longer depend on iodized salt to get enough of the trace element in our diets.

You probably have heard of fleur de sel, lovely finishing salts that are hand harvested along the coast of western France. Fleur de sel is expensive, no doubt about it, but remember it's not meant for anything but scattering on food just before eating. It's crunchy, mild saltiness brings out the flavors of grilled vegetables, poultry, and fish, as well as tomatoes and green salads. It's a waste of money to use it for anything else. Don't sprinkle it in the pasta water or add it to a simmering stew.

At Aux Délices, we sell a number of specialty salts, all fun to try now and then. Smoked sea salt, coconut and lime sea salt, sea salt with African spices, sea salt with herbs all are found on our shelves. Lots of salt aficionados like flake salts, with the best-known being Maldon sea salt, harvested along England's coastline. There also are gray and red salts from Hawaii, salts from parts of Asia, including the Himalayas, and flaked sea salt from Cyprus—to name a few. All these fancy salts are meant as finishing salts.

For everyday use, reach for kosher or sea salt.

EASY BEEF STEW

I wanted to come up with a recipe for beef stew that wasn't intimidating, although when you look at the long list of ingredients you might be tempted to turn the page. Please don't! Once you assemble the stew meat and vegetables, the rest is easy. The stew cooks for about an hour and then it's ready. If you make it a day ahead and reheat it before serving, it's even better—and even easier come dinnertime.

Serves 4

2 pounds beef stew meat, such as top round or chuck

Kosher salt and freshly ground black pepper

2 to 3 tablespoons canola oil

6 slices bacon, cut into ¼-inch pieces

2 tablespoons unsalted butter

1 small onion, diced

4 garlic cloves, sliced

2 tablespoons all-purpose flour

1 bottle red wine

4 carrots, peeled and cut into large dice

8 ounces mushrooms, cleaned and halved

8 ounces pearl or cippolini onions

1 cup chicken stock, preferably homemade

2 tablespoons tomato paste

2 bay leaves

1 tablespoon chopped fresh thyme

1 teaspoon chopped fresh rosemary

1 cup frozen peas, thawed

¼ cup chopped flat-leaf parsley

Season the stew meat with salt and pepper.

In a heavy Dutch oven or similar heavy pot, heat 2 tablespoons of oil over medium-high heat until shimmering. Sear the beef in batches until golden brown on all sides. Transfer the browned meat to a platter or bowl as it's done.

Add the bacon and the rest of the oil, if the pot seems dry, and sauté until the fat is rendered and the bacon is crispy. Add the butter and when it melts, add the onion and garlic and cook, stirring occasionally, for 4 to 5 minutes until the onion soften.

Sprinkle the flour over the bacon mixture and cook for 1 minute longer, stirring constantly and scraping the bottom of the pan to remove any browned bits.

Add the wine and cook over medium-high heat for about 5 minutes, stirring occasionally and scraping the bottom of the pot. Skim any foam that rises to the top of the pot.

Add the carrots, mushrooms, pearl onions, stock, tomato paste, bay leaves, thyme, rosemary, and the browned meat. Bring to a boil, skim any foam that rises to the top, and then reduce the heat and simmer for 50 to 60 minutes, or until the meat is tender. Adjust the heat as needed to maintain a gentle simmer.

Finally, stir in the peas and parsley and season to taste with salt and pepper. Serve the stew hot.

MOROCCAN LAMB STEW

My husband told me this might be his favorite recipe in the entire book, which is ironic since he has never been a fan of lamb stews. There is something about the mixture of spices, including cinnamon and cumin, that deepens the flavors. As wonderful as the spices are together, if you're missing one, don't let that stop you from making the stew. I really like the orange rind finish, but you can omit it if it seems too fussy. You also could substitute dried apricots for the dates. Just make it! Serve it with the Golden Almond Couscous on page 224 and a green salad for a lovely meal. One caveat: like so many stews and braises, this is best if made a day ahead of time and reheated.

Serves 4

2 teaspoons paprika

1 teaspoon caraway seeds

1 tablespoon ground cumin

1 teaspoon ground coriander seeds

1 teaspoon curry powder

Kosher salt and freshly ground black pepper

2 ½ pounds lamb stew meat, cut into 1-inch pieces

5 tablespoons canola oil

3 carrots, peeled and cut into medium dice

1 onion, cut into medium dice

4 garlic cloves, thinly sliced

2 cups red wine

2 bay leaves

2 cinnamon sticks

2 cups beef stock, preferably homemade (or one 14.5-ounce can)

2 cups crushed canned tomatoes

½ cup Kalamata olives, pitted and diced

6 Medjool dates, pitted and diced

2 pieces orange rind, each about 3-inches long and ½-inch thick

Stir together the paprika, caraway seeds, cumin, coriander, curry powder, and 2 teaspoons of salt. Season with a few grinds of pepper.

Spread the lamb pieces on a work surface and sprinkle evenly with the spice mixture. Take care to coat all the meat.

In a heavy, lidded pot or Dutch oven, heat 2 tablespoons of the oil over medium-high heat until almost smoking. In two batches, sear the lamb, turning it to brown on all sides. As the meat is browned, transfer it to a plate.

Add the remaining 3 tablespoons of oil to the pan, lower the heat to medium, and cook the carrots, onion, and garlic, stirring occasionally, for 5 to 8 minutes or until the onion softens.

Add the red wine, bay leaves, and cinnamon sticks and bring to a boil over medium-high heat. Lower the heat and simmer for 5 minutes.

Return the lamb to the pot and add the stock and tomatoes. Bring to a boil over medium-high heat and skim any foam that rises to the surface.

Reduce the heat to low, cover the pot, and cook for about 1 hour. Uncover the pot, skimming again if necessary, and cook uncovered for 35 minutes, stirring occasionally, or until the lamb is very tender, with no lingering toughness and the flavors are nicely melded. Add the olives, dates, and orange rinds. Remove and discard the cinnamon and bay leaves. Season to taste with salt and pepper and serve.

CHAPTER 6

PASTA AND BEYOND

I MARRIED INTO AN ITALIAN AMERICAN FAMILY AND BY NOW HAVE HAPPILY EMBRACED MANY OF THE CULINARY TRADITIONS SO BELOVED BY THE CULTURE, INCLUDING A PASSION FOR PASTA. But in the early years of my marriage, I didn't get it. What was so special about pasta? After years of family gatherings where at least two or more pasta dishes always showed up as part of the buffet, I became a true believer. Greg and I also like to travel in Italy whenever we can (never often enough) where I spend mad happy days trying every pasta dish I can. I am a pasta nut. The recipes in this chapter rank as favorites in our household. If you find yourself cooking pasta two or three times a week, as so many moms and dads do, the recipes here will help you change it up. Take my word for it: once you try my pasta gnocchi, you will never be wary of making gnocchi again. Some recipes are directly influenced by those I sampled in Italy, others, like the Baked Mac and Cheese, are firmly more American in style. And some are fusion: for example, I recently started using parboiled lasagna sheets for the first time and promptly became a devout convert.

BAKED MAC AND CHEESE

A young American chef I know who studied in London passed this recipe along to me. I made it my own but essentially I learned to make this very American dish from someone trained by the Brits. Of course, the English make some of the best Cheddar cheese on the planet, and the better and sharper the cheese, the better the final dish. The milk stirred with the cheese makes the sauce especially creamy, although there is no cream in the recipe.

Serves 8

4 tablespoons unsalted butter

5 leeks, trimmed, white and pale green parts, cut into half-moon slices (about 5 cups)

3 tablespoons all-purpose flour

4 cups milk

12 ounces sharp Cheddar cheese, grated (about 4 cups)

2 teaspoons Dijon mustard

2 teaspoons kosher salt

Freshly ground black pepper

1 pound penne

Preheat the oven to 400°F. Spray a 13 x 9 x 2-inch baking dish with cooking spray.

Melt the butter in a large saucepan and cook the leeks, covered, for 10 to 12 minutes, or until they are softened but have no color.

Uncover the pan, sprinkle the flour over the leeks, and continue to cook for about 1 minute longer, stirring constantly. Add 3 1/2 cups of the milk, bring to a boil, reduce the heat, and stir in 3 cups of the cheese and the mustard. Remove the pan from the heat and stir until the cheese melts and the sauce is smooth. Add the salt and season to taste with the pepper.

Meanwhile, cook the pasta according to package directions so that it is al dente. Drain well, add the pasta to the cheese sauce, and then gently stir in the remaining 1/2 cup of milk. Pour the pasta into the prepared baking dish, top with the remaining cup of cheese, and bake for 25 to 30 minutes until just golden brown. Serve hot.

When Pasta Is Just Pasta

When I first wrote down the pasta recipes for this book, I tended to say things like "1 pound pasta" rather than "1 pound rigatoni" or "$1/2$ cup penne." This is because there are times when pasta is just pasta. For example, you can substitute ziti for penne and get great results. But when I realized some folks may try to replace the penne with linguine, I decided to make the recipes more specific.

I think it's interesting to note that the various pasta shapes were invented to work with different sauces. Chunky sauces go best with chubby, thick pastas such as penne and farfalle, while smooth, creamy sauces are better suited for ribbons of pasta such as fettuccini, linguine, and spaghetti. This is because the little pieces of meat or vegetables will lodge in the nooks and crevices created by the stubbier pastas, but will slide off the ribbony strands.

Speaking of sauces, don't neglect the pasta cooking water, which is a little starchy once the pasta has cooked in it. It can both thin and add body to a sauce, and works exceptionally well with simple, light ones. It extends these sauces without the need for more oil, butter, or cheese, which may be too much for light coatings.

So, while pasta is just pasta most of the time, it's the shape and not the name that matters most when you select the right noodle for a dish.

LAMB RAGU
WITH RIGATONI

One of my favorite ways to serve pasta is to toss it with meat ragus, and this one, made with lamb, meets my highest expectations. Lamb, so earthy and robust, stands up to the relatively long cooking time required for braising, but because I use ground lamb, it's done in about 45 minutes. This means you can make this rigatoni any day, even on a busy weeknight.

Serves 4

2 tablespoons extra-virgin olive oil, plus more as needed

1 pound ground lamb

1 celery rib, finely diced

1 carrot, peeled and finely diced

½ onion, finely minced

Kosher salt and freshly ground black pepper

1 tablespoon tomato paste

¾ cup red wine

1 cup whole canned tomatoes, plus ½ cup of the juice

1½ cups chicken stock, preferably homemade

1 teaspoon chopped fresh rosemary

1 bay leaf

½ teaspoon chopped fresh thyme

½ teaspoon ground coriander

½ teaspoon cumin

1 pound rigatoni

½ cup grated Parmesan cheese

Heat the oil in a deep sauté pan over medium-high heat and when hot, cook the lamb, breaking it up with a wooden spoon as it browns. When the lamb is browned, add the celery, carrot, and onion and cook, stirring, for 2 to 3 minutes. Season to taste with salt and pepper.

Add the tomato paste and cook for about 1 minute. Add the red wine and cook, stirring, for 3 to 4 minutes, or until the ragu is thick and most of the wine has evaporated. Add the canned tomatoes, breaking them up with your fingers as they go in the pan. Stir in the tomato juice and the stock. Add the rosemary, bay leaf, thyme, coriander, and cumin.

Reduce the heat and simmer the ragu for about 45 minutes, or until it thickens. Season with about $^1/_2$ teaspoon of salt and pepper. Remove and discard the bay leaf.

Cook the rigatoni according to package directions. Drain, toss the hot pasta with a little olive oil, and season with salt and pepper. Spoon the pasta into individual pasta bowls and top with the lamb ragu. Serve sprinkled with Parmesan cheese.

LINGUINE WITH GREEN BEANS AND POTATOES

I ate this classic last year when I was in Italy and urged everyone at the table to sample a little. It was universally beloved at first bite, although we joked about how only the Italians would think of mixing potatoes with pasta—and how only Americans would consider it a carb overload! Never mind: The balance of flavors and ingredients is just about perfect and cooking the pasta in the same water as the green beans saves a pot, too. This has become a real family favorite.

Serves 6

1 pound red bliss potatoes or white creamer potatoes

Kosher salt

1 pound haricots verts or string beans, trimmed

1 pound trenette or linguine

2 to 3 tablespoons olive oil

Freshly ground black pepper

Basil Pesto (recipe follows)

Put the potatoes in a saucepan, cover with cold water and sprinkle generously with salt. Bring to a boil over medium-high heat, reduce the heat, and simmer for 25 to 30 minutes, or until fork-tender. Drain the potatoes and when cool, cut them into thin slices. This can be done a few hours ahead of time.

Bring a large pot of salted water to a boil over medium-high heat and cook the haricots verts for about 5 minutes or until tender. Remove with a slotted spoon and set aside. Let the water return to the boil, add the pasta, and cook according to the package directions. Before draining the pasta, remove about a cup of the cooking liquid. Drain the pasta.

In a large sauté pan, heat 2 tablespoons of the olive oil over medium-high heat and when shimmering, sauté the sliced potatoes for about 1 minute. Add the remaining tablespoon of oil if needed. Season to taste with salt and pepper.

Add the beans, at least 1 cup of the pesto, the pasta, and enough of the reserved pasta cooking water to make it a smooth sauce. Taste and adjust the seasoning with salt and pepper and add more pesto, if desired.

BASIL PESTO

3 cups fresh basil leaves

²/₃ cup extra-virgin olive oil

¹/₄ cup Parmesan cheese

2 whole garlic cloves, peeled

2 tablespoons pine nuts

¹/₂ teaspoon kosher salt

Freshly ground black pepper

Put the basil, olive oil, cheese, garlic, pine nuts, and salt in a food processor and process to a smooth paste. Season to taste with pepper and pulse briefly. The pesto can be made 2 to 3 days ahead of time and refrigerated until needed.

RICOTTA GNOCCHI WITH SUMMER CORN AND PEAS

I am practically a weekly gnocchi maker. No one can believe I make it so often as a weeknight meal, but they have no idea how simple it is. This pasta recipe is lighter and easier than the more traditional potato gnocchi, and because it's made with smooth ricotta, it whips up in a flash. It's great sautéed with seasonal vegetables, as here, and if you are pressed for time, it's fantastic with marinara sauce or a brown butter and sage sauce.

Serves 4

GNOCCHI

15 ounces whole-milk ricotta

2 large egg yolks

1 1/2 teaspoons salt

1 cup all-purpose flour

2 tablespoons Parmesan cheese

Freshly ground black pepper

2 tablespoons extra-virgin olive oil

VEGETABLES

2 tablespoons unsalted butter

2 cups fresh corn kernels (from 3 to 4 ears of corn)

(continued)

TO MAKE THE GNOCCHI: Mix together the ricotta, egg yolks, and salt with a wooden spoon until blended. Stir in the flour and Parmesan until the mixture forms a sticky dough. Turn out onto a well-floured surface and knead until smooth. Divide the dough into four pieces.

Sprinkle a little more flour on the work surface and roll each piece of dough into 1/2-inch-thick ropes that are 6 to 8 inches long. Cut into pieces, each about 1/2 inch long. Set the pieces of dough on a clean, dry baking sheet as they are cut. This can be done 2 or 3 hours ahead of time.

Bring a large pot of water to a boil over medium-high heat. Sprinkle it generously with salt and add some of the gnocchi. I use a large slotted spoon and cook two to three scoopfuls at a time. The trick is not to crowd the pan. Stir the pot gently and occasionally as the gnocchi boil gently for 1 to 1 1/2 minutes. The gnocchi are done when they rise to the top. Remove them from the pot with a slotted spoon and transfer them to a lightly oiled baking pan and sprinkle them lightly with olive oil. Continue to cook the rest

1 cup fresh or frozen peas, blanched

1 teaspoon chopped fresh thyme

Kosher salt and freshly ground black pepper

of the gnocchi. Sprinkle with oil. Make sure the water returns to the boil between batches.

TO COOK THE CORN AND PEAS: Melt the butter over medium heat in a large sauté pan and when bubbly, add the corn and sauté for about 5 minutes or until tender. Stir in the peas and thyme and the gnocchi, season to taste with salt and pepper, toss gently, and heat through (you may need two sauté pans). Serve at once.

SIMPLE SPAGHETTI WITH ARUGULA AND PARMESAN

What could be easier than this spaghetti dish? If you're like me and love arugula, chances are you will have all the ingredients on hand and can devise this meal at the drop of a hat. If not, it's worth the trip to the market to stock up on the peppery bitter green and some great Parmesan cheese. They love this in Italy—which is recommendation enough for me!

Serves 4 to 6

1 pound spaghetti

¹/₃ cup extra-virgin olive oil

1 tablespoon unsalted butter

4 garlic cloves, sliced

¹/₄ to ¹/₂ teaspoon dried red pepper flakes

8 loosely packed cups baby arugula (about 1 pound)

¹/₄ cup roughly chopped flat-leaf parsley (about a quarter of a bunch)

¹/₂ cup grated Parmesan cheese, plus extra for serving

Kosher salt and freshly ground black pepper

Bring a large pot of salted water to a boil over medium-high heat and cook the spaghetti according to the package directions. Before draining, reserve 1 cup of the pasta cooking water.

Heat the olive oil and butter in a large skillet over medium heat and when the butter is bubbling, reduce the heat to low and sauté the garlic for 1 to 2 minutes or until nearly golden brown. Add the red pepper flakes and sauté for a few seconds. Add the drained spaghetti to the skillet along with the arugula, parsley, and about ³/₄ cup of the reserved pasta water. Mix well.

Add the Parmesan and toss until well mixed and heated through. Add a little more pasta water or olive oil if the pasta seems dry. Season to taste with salt and pepper and serve with more grated Parmesan cheese on the side.

QUICK PASTA WITH BASIL AND LEMON

As a true lemon lover, I am a big fan of this combo of lemon and basil with pasta and grated cheese. Another thing I love about it is that you probably have most of the ingredients in your refrigerator and some fresh basil in the garden (or a pot on the windowsill). If not, you will have to stop by the market but luckily fresh basil is pretty easy to find. This could turn into a very special main course with some grilled shrimp on top.

Serves 4

1 pound spaghetti or linguine

1 tablespoon unsalted butter

½ cup olive oil

Juice of 2 lemons (about ¼ cup)

Grated zest of ½ lemon

1¼ cups grated Parmesan cheese

1 cup basil leaves cut in a chiffonade (see note)

Kosher salt and freshly ground black pepper

Bring a large pot of salted water to a boil over medium-high heat and cook the spaghetti according to the package directions. Before draining, reserve about ½ cup of the pasta cooking water. Drain the pasta, return it to the pot, and add the butter. Toss until the butter melts and coats the pasta.

Meanwhile, whisk together the olive oil, lemon juice, lemon zest, and Parmesan cheese. Toss this with the buttered pasta and add some of the reserved pasta water to loosen it up a little.

Add the basil and toss gently. Season to taste with salt and pepper and serve right away.

NOTE: To cut the basil leaves in a chiffonade, stack them on top of each other, roll the stack like a cigar, and slice thinly across the cylinder.

CLASSIC CHEESE LASAGNA

As someone who never used parboiled pasta sheets until I cooked this recipe for the book, let me assure you: I am a convert! And like many converts, I am wildly enthusiastic about my discovery. The noodles allow you to whip up a lasagna with little fuss or muss. You can build the casserole shortly before a weeknight supper, and it's even better if you make the lasagna in the morning, keep it refrigerated, and then pop it in the oven an hour before supper. Just be sure to cover the pasta sheets with sauce so they stay nice and moist.

Serves 10 to 12

3 cups shredded mozzarella cheese (about 9 ounces)

1 pound whole milk ricotta cheese

1 cup grated Asiago cheese (about 3 ounces)

½ cup grated Parmesan cheese

3 large egg yolks

½ cup chopped flat-leaf parsley (about half a bunch)

1 teaspoon kosher salt

Freshly ground black pepper

6 cups marinara sauce, homemade or your favorite jarred brand

1 pound no-boil lasagna noodles

1 pound fresh mozzarella, thinly sliced

Preheat the oven to 350°F.

Mix together 1 cup of the shredded mozzarella, ricotta, Asiago, and Parmesan cheeses. Add the egg yolks, parsley, and salt. Season to taste with pepper and stir until smooth.

Spread 1 cup of marinara sauce over the bottom of a 12 x 8-inch lasagna or similar baking pan. Layer the noodles over the sauce and then dollop about 1 cup of the cheese mixture over the noodles and spread in as even a layer as possible. Take care to cover the noodles completely.

Repeat the process with another cup of sauce, another layer of noodles and another cup of the cheese mixture. Shingle a layer of sliced fresh mozzarella over the top of the cheese mixture. Top with another cup of sauce and layer of pasta. Spoon another cup of the cheese mixture over the pasta, spread it evenly, and then add another cup of sauce. Lay more noodles over the sauce and spoon the remaining cup of the cheese mixture over them. Spread it evenly and top with the remaining slices of fresh mozzarella. Top with the final 2 cups of sauce and then the remaining 2 cups of shredded mozzarella.

Cover the lasagna loosely with aluminum foil and bake for about 50 minutes. Remove the foil and return the pan to the oven for another 15 minutes, or until the cheese is melted and golden brown. Allow the lasagna to cool for 10 to 15 minutes before cutting and serving.

FARFALLE WITH ZUCCHINI AND CLAMS

When I travel in Italy, I order this over and over and am never disappointed. You can skip the thyme if you want, but don't skimp on the parsley. And just before serving be sure to finish the dish with extra-virgin olive oil. My best advice for this is to be sure to start with a pot big enough to hold the clams, zucchini, and pasta.

Serves 6

4 zucchini (1½ pounds total)

¼ cup, plus 2 tablespoons olive oil

4 shallots, sliced

2 garlic cloves, finely sliced

1 teaspoon chopped fresh thyme

2½ pounds littleneck clams

¼ cup clam juice

½ cup white wine

1 pound farfalle

2 tablespoons unsalted butter

¼ to ½ teaspoon dried red pepper flakes (or to taste)

¼ cup chopped flat-leaf parsley

Kosher salt and freshly ground black pepper

Trim the ends of the zucchini, slice in half lengthwise, and cut into ½-inch-thick half-moon slices.

In a large sauté pan with a tight-fitting lid, heat the 2 tablespoons of olive oil over medium-high heat until shimmering. Reduce the heat to medium-low and cook the shallots and garlic, stirring, for 2 to 3 minutes or until tender.

Raise the heat to medium and cook the zucchini and thyme for about 5 to 6 minutes or until the zucchini is just tender.

Add the clams, clam juice, and wine, cover tightly, and cook over medium heat for 4 to 5 minutes or until the clams open. Stir the clams and zucchini once or twice during steaming.

Meanwhile, cook the pasta according to package directions until al dente. Drain and transfer the pasta to the pan with the clams and zucchini. Add the remaining ¼ cup of olive oil, butter, red pepper flakes, and parsley and toss gently over medium heat until the butter melts and the ingredients are nicely mixed. Season to taste with salt and pepper.

RIGATONI WITH CARAMELIZED ONIONS AND ROASTED TOMATOES

There is something about the marriage of sweet, caramelized onions and tangy goat cheese that pleases many a palate. I sampled a quesadilla made with these ingredients and was charmed by the flavors. I knew they would be wonderful with rigatoni. Toss some roasted tomatoes into the mix and you have an amazing creamy-tangy-sweet pasta dish. Love it!

Serves 4

¼ cup olive oil

2 medium-size red onions, very thinly sliced

1 teaspoon chopped fresh thyme leaves

2 pints cherry or grape tomatoes

Kosher salt and freshly ground black pepper

3 sprigs fresh thyme

2 tablespoons extra-virgin olive oil

1 pound rigatoni

6 ounces goat cheese, crumbled

1 small bunch chives, minced

Preheat the oven to 325°F.

Heat the ¼ cup of olive oil in a medium-size saucepan over medium-high heat. Reduce the heat to low and cook the onions and chopped thyme, stirring occasionally, for 30 to 35 minutes, or until softened and caramelized.

Toss the cherry tomatoes with a good sprinkling of salt and pepper, and the thyme sprigs and spread them in a small, shallow baking pan. Roast for about 30 minutes without stirring, or until the tomatoes are slightly blistered and softened.

Bring a large pot of salted water to a boil over medium-high heat and cook the pasta according to the package directions. Before draining, reserve about ¼ cup of the pasta cooking water. Drain the pasta and return it to the pot. Add the 2 tablespoons of extra-virgin olive oil and then fold in the caramelized onions.

Gently mix the cherry tomatoes with the pasta. Discard the thyme sprigs. Next, gently stir in the goat cheese and a little of the pasta water to loosen the pasta, if needed. Stir in the chives, season to taste with salt and pepper, and serve right away.

PASTA WITH WALNUT RICOTTA PESTO

I find a lot of pasta dishes addictive and this one especially so. It's hard to let even a little bit remain clinging to the side of the pan. The first time I made this, I didn't tell my family that there were walnuts in the sauce, fearing they would turn up their noses. They cleaned their plates and asked for seconds.

Serves 4 to 6

1 pound pasta, such as penne

2 tablespoons unsalted butter, softened

1 cup frozen peas, thawed

3 ounces prosciutto, very thinly sliced

Kosher salt and freshly ground black pepper

Walnut Pesto (recipe follows)

Cook the pasta according to package directions until al dente. Before draining, reserve about $1/4$ cup of the pasta water. Add the pasta to the pesto and mix well. Mix the pasta water into the pasta if the pesto seems too thick, adding it a tablespoon at a time.

Gently toss in the butter, peas, and prosciutto. Season to taste with salt and pepper and serve right away.

WALNUT PESTO

Makes 2 generous cups

1 1/2 cups walnut pieces, toasted

2 garlic cloves

1 cup ricotta cheese

1/4 cup grated Parmesan cheese

1/4 cup extra-virgin olive oil

1/4 cup chopped flat-leaf parsley

1 teaspoon kosher salt

In the bowl of a food processor, process the walnuts and garlic until finely ground. Scrape into a serving bowl and add the ricotta cheese, Parmesan cheese, olive oil, parsley, and salt. Mix well and set aside at room temperature.

EVERYBODY LOVES BURGERS

BURGERS ARE PRACTICALLY A NATIONAL PASTIME.

We flip them on the backyard grill, fry them up in large skillets, and rely on them to sustain us when we're out and about. I'm as loyal to burgers as anyone, and these days I am happy there are so many options for them beyond beef. Don't misunderstand me: I love a good beef burger, but I'm a fan of others, too.

Most of all, a good burger is dependent on great bread, condiments, sauces, and toppings. Without these, a burger is just a cooked patty—and that's no fun. And so, regardless of what's in the burger—meat, seafood, turkey, or veggies—pay attention to the trimmings. Try one of these burgers every week for the next month and see how your family responds. If they are anything like mine, they will be only too happy to come to the table and dig in.

You can serve the burgers with the accompaniments I suggest in the recipes, which I think make them the best they can be. Or, rely on normal trappings: lettuce, tomatoes, pickles, ketchup, mustard. For something a little more adventurous, go for the Oven-Baked Fries with Parmesan and Rosemary on page 221 or the Sweet Potato Salad with Mango on page 29 to serve alongside.

MEATLOAF BURGERS

If you like meatloaf as much as I do—and if you are reading this recipe, you probably do—you will love these. I mix beef, pork, and veal together to intensify the flavor. These are often packaged as "meatloaf mix" or something similar. If your market doesn't do this, buy the meats separately. If you have a butcher, ask him to grind the meat for you.

Serves 6

2 tablespoons olive oil

1 small onion, very finely diced

1 rib celery, finely diced

3 garlic cloves, minced

1 1/2-pound package lean ground beef, pork, and veal (if these are not sold packaged together, buy 1/2 pound of each)

1/2 cup fresh breadcrumbs

1 tablespoon tomato paste

1 tablespoon Worcestershire sauce

1/3 cup ketchup, plus 6 tablespoons

2 teaspoons salt

Freshly ground black pepper

6 hamburger buns

Preheat the oven to 375°F.

Heat the oil in a skillet over medium-high heat until shimmering and cook the onion, celery, and garlic for about 5 minutes, or until softened. Set aside to cool.

Mix together the meat, breadcrumbs, tomato paste, Worcestershire sauce, 1/3 cup of ketchup, and salt. Season with pepper. Add the cooled vegetables and mix well, using your hands or a wooden spoon.

Shape the meat into six patties and arrange on a baking sheet. Spread 1 tablespoon of ketchup on each burger and bake for about 25 minutes or until cooked through.

Serve tucked inside the hamburger buns.

SLOPPY JOES

Sloppy Joes sound like kid fare, and while children are all about this dish, my recipe has some very adult flourishes such as the Dijon mustard. Serve it with sliced red onion, shredded Cheddar or jack cheese, a dollop of sour cream, and some sliced avocado for decidedly grown-up touches. This is a quick, easy, under-30-minutes recipe that your whole family will love.

Serves 4

1 tablespoon olive oil

1 pound lean ground beef

1 garlic clove, minced

3/4 cup ketchup

1 (6-ounce) can tomato paste

1 tablespoon Dijon mustard

2 packed teaspoons brown sugar

3/4 teaspoon chili powder

1 teaspoon salt

Freshly ground black pepper

4 hamburger buns

Heat the oil in a skillet over medium-high heat until hot and cook the beef and garlic, stirring with a wooden spoon, until the beef is no longer pink. Remove the beef from the pan with a slotted spoon and pour off the fat. Return the beef to the pan and add the ketchup, tomato paste, mustard, brown sugar, and chili powder. Stir well, add 3/4 cup water, and cook over medium-low heat for 5 to 6 minutes or until everything is combined and slightly thickened. Add the salt and season to taste with pepper. Spoon the warm Sloppy Joe filling over the hamburger buns.

BACON BURGERS WITH FRIED EGGS AND PESTO MAYONNAISE

I am the first to admit this burger is way over the top. Eggs and bacon? Mayonnaise? All served with a juicy beef burger? This may not fall into the "healthful" category but is has an honored place on my Top 10 Burgers list in terms of pure deliciousness! In fact, when I was done testing and retesting the recipes destined for the pages of this book, my kids begged for the bacon and egg burgers "one more time, please!" So, if you feel like splurging on an extreme burger, here is your chance.

Serves 4

¼ cup mayonnaise

¼ cup Basil Pesto (page 151)

Kosher salt and freshly ground black pepper

1½ pounds lean ground beef

4 hamburger buns

8 slices lean bacon, cooked until crisp and drained

2 tablespoons canola oil

4 large eggs

Mix together the mayonnaise and pesto, season with salt and pepper, and set aside.

Season the beef with salt and pepper and shape the meat into four patties.

Preheat the grill to medium hot. Grill the patties for 3 to 4 minutes on each side or until they reach the desired degree of doneness.

Spread a generous tablespoon of the pesto mayonnaise on the bottom halves of the hamburger buns and lay two slices of bacon on each bun. Put a burger on top of the bacon.

Heat the oil in a medium sauté pan over medium heat. (You may find it easier to cook the eggs in two pans, two eggs per pan.) Crack the eggs in a small bowl one at a time and carefully slide each one into the pan. Season with salt and pepper, cover, and cook for about 2 minutes or until the whites are opaque. Lift the fried eggs from the pan and put 1 egg on top of each burger. Top with the remaining halves of the buns and serve right away.

GREEK LAMB BURGERS

Ground lamb doesn't get any respect; it's often a forgotten meat at the butcher counter. If you like the full, rich flavor of lamb, these burgers are out of the world. The tzatziki, made with thick yogurt and fresh mint leaves, is the crowning touch.

Serves 4

1 pound ground lamb

¼ onion, grated (about ½ cup)

1 garlic clove, minced

1 large egg

15 Kalamata olives, pitted and chopped

1¼ teaspoons salt

1 teaspoon chopped fresh oregano

¾ teaspoon ground cumin

3 ounces feta cheese, crumbled

Freshly ground black pepper

2 tablespoons canola oil

4 pita pockets or pieces of na'an

4 slices fresh, ripe tomato

Mix together the lamb, onion, garlic, egg, olives, salt, oregano, and cumin. When well mixed, gently fold the feta cheese into the mixture and season with pepper. Form the meat into four patties.

Heat the oil in a medium sauté pan over medium-high heat and when shimmering, cook the patties for 4 to 5 minutes on each side or until cooked to your desired degree of doneness.

Serve each burger tucked in the pita pockets or na'an with a tomato slice. Top each burger with a good tablespoon of tzatziki.

MINT TZATZIKI

Makes about 1 cup

3/4 cup nonfat Greek yogurt

1 cucumber, peeled,
 seeded, and finely diced

1 garlic clove, minced

1 tablespoon chopped
fresh mint leaves

1 teaspoon apple cider
vinegar

Kosher salt and freshly
ground black pepper

Mix together the yogurt, cucumber, garlic, mint leaves, and vinegar. Season to taste with salt and pepper. Set aside in the refrigerator if not using soon.

SOUTHWESTERN TURKEY BURGERS

In growing numbers of American households, turkey burgers are the burgers of choice—or at least some of the time. Many of us try to eat less beef, and so ground turkey has inched its way onto the culinary stage, although still playing a minor role. When you mix the turkey with flavors inspired by the dishes of the Southwest like cilantro, adobo sauce, and cumin, and then serve the burgers with pepper jack cheese and some sliced avocado, no one misses the more familiar beef burger.

Serves 4

1 pound ground turkey

2 scallions, trimmed and sliced thinly on the bias, white and light green parts

1 garlic clove, minced

½ cup chopped cilantro

½ cup finely minced red bell pepper

2 tablespoons adobo sauce (from a can of chipotle peppers in adobo)

2 tablespoons canola oil, plus more for cooking

1 teaspoon salt

½ teaspoon cumin

Freshly ground pepper

4 slices pepper jack cheese

4 hamburger buns

Guacamole or sliced avocado for garnish (optional)

Mix together the turkey, scallions, garlic, cilantro, red pepper, adobo sauce, oil, salt, and cumin. Season with pepper. Form the mixture into four patties.

Heat the oil in a medium sauté pan over medium-high heat and when shimmering, cook the patties for about 4 minutes on each side or until cooked through. Just before lifting the burgers from the pan, top each with a slice of cheese and let it melt.

Serve the burgers on the hamburger buns, topped with guacamole or avocado slices, if desired.

GINGERED SALMON BURGERS

A great change from roasted or grilled salmon, these burgers are not only tasty, but super-easy to make. I season them with a touch of garlic, ginger, and hoisin—the Asian accent adds to their overall appeal. These are great with or without buns, and if you want them to go bunless, top them with the Vegetables in Sesame Vinaigrette on page 121.

Serves 4

1¼ pounds skinless salmon fillet, cut into 1-inch pieces

4 scallions, trimmed and thinly sliced

1 garlic clove, minced

3 tablespoons minced fresh, peeled ginger

3 tablespoons hoisin sauce

1 teaspoon kosher salt, plus more for seasoning

Freshly ground black pepper

2 tablespoons canola oil

4 hamburger buns

About 2 tablespoons mayonnaise

4 slices tomato

4 slices red onion

4 lettuce leaves

Put the salmon, scallions, garlic, ginger, hoisin sauce, and 1 teaspoon of salt in a food processor and process until smooth. Season to taste with pepper and pulse to mix.

Form the mixture into four patties and season lightly with salt and pepper.

In a large sauté pan, heat the oil over medium heat until shimmering and cook the salmon burgers for 3 to 4 minutes on each side or just until cooked through. Lower the heat during cooking if the marinade remaining on the burgers starts to caramelize.

Spread the hamburger buns with mayonnaise and top with a salmon burger. Top the burgers with tomato, onion, and lettuce and serve.

CAJUN CRAB BURGERS

What's the difference between a crab burger and a crab cake? I am not sure there is much, but these are little more robust than the crab cakes on page 54, and I serve them in nice soft potato buns, which work best with seafood burgers. I once served these at a Super Bowl party to great applause; everyone responded happily to the South Louisiana spices in the crab mixture and the mayo. When making crab burgers or crab cakes, always start with top-notch crabmeat. And if you form and chill these ahead of time, not only will life be easier when it's time to cook them, they will hold together a little better in the hot oil. To save even more time at the last minute, cook these ahead of time and reheat them in the oven, arranged in a shallow baking pan.

Serves 6

1 tablespoon unsalted butter

½ cup minced yellow onion

½ cup minced celery

½ cup minced green bell pepper

1 garlic clove, minced

⅓ cup mayonnaise

1 large egg

1 tablespoon Worcestershire sauce

1 tablespoon Dijon mustard

1½ teaspoons Cajun seasoning

1 teaspoon hot pepper sauce

(continued)

In a medium sauté pan, melt the butter over medium heat. Add the onion, celery, pepper, and garlic and cook for 4 to 5 minutes, or until the vegetables soften. Set aside to cool.

Whisk together the mayonnaise, egg, Worcestershire sauce, mustard, Cajun seasoning, hot pepper sauce, and paprika. Stir the cooled vegetables into the mixture and then gently toss in the crab to combine. Fold in 1 cup of the breadcrumbs and season to taste with salt and pepper.

Form the crab mixture into six patties, each about ½-inch thick. Coat with the remaining breadcrumbs and if not cooking right away, refrigerate for up 4 hours. (These are a little easier to cook when chilled, but it's not necessary.)

In a large sauté pan, heat enough oil to come halfway up the sides of the crab patties. Heat the oil over medium-high heat or until a breadcrumb sizzles when dropped in the oil.

½ teaspoon paprika

1 pound lump crabmeat

1½ to 1¾ cups fresh
breadcrumbs (see note)

Kosher salt and freshly
ground black pepper

Canola oil, for frying

6 potato rolls or hamburger
rolls

Creole Mayonnaise
(recipe follows)

Gently lower the crab patties into the oil using a slotted spoon and cook for 4 to 5 minutes on each side or until golden brown.

Serve on the rolls and top each burger with Creole Mayonnaise.

NOTE: To make fresh breadcrumbs, grind bread in a blender or food processor until it turns into crumbs. For more, see page 55.

CREOLE MAYONNAISE

Makes a generous ½ cup

½ cup mayonnaise

1 tablespoon Worcestershire
sauce

1 teaspoon Dijon mustard

1 teaspoon Cajun seasoning

A few drops fresh lemon
juice

Kosher salt and freshly
ground black pepper

Whisk the mayonnaise with the Worcestershire sauce, mustard, Cajun seasoning, and lemon juice. Season to taste with salt and pepper and more lemon juice, if needed.

Use right away or cover and refrigerate for up to 4 days.

OPEN-FACED GRILLED PORTOBELLO MUSHROOMS ON SOURDOUGH

Not all burgers are created equal, and some don't even contain meat or poultry. I love using a big, meaty portobello mushroom as the base for a grilled veggie burger made with melted Muenster, a cheese that is super-friendly to the mushrooms. While you could substitute another cheese, I urge you to try Muenster for an amazing taste experience.

Serves 4

4 portobello mushroom caps

Generous ½ cup olive oil

4 slices red onion, each about ¼-inch thick

4 slices tomato, each about ½-inch thick

4 slices sourdough bread, each about ½-inch thick

Kosher salt and freshly ground black pepper

4 slices Muenster cheese, each about ¼-inch thick, or another good melting cheese such as Havarti or jack

¼ cup Basil Pesto (page 151)

Preheat a gas or charcoal grill to medium hot.

Drizzle the inside of each mushroom cap with about 1 tablespoon of olive oil. Brush the onion, tomato, and bread slices with the remaining oil.

Put the mushrooms on the grill, oiled sides down, and grill for about 3 minutes. Add the onion slices to the grill, season lightly with salt and pepper, and grill for about 3 minutes longer. Turn over both the mushroom caps and the onions, season again with salt and pepper, and continue to grill for about 3 minutes longer.

Lay a slice of cheese over each mushroom cap so that it can melt into the mushroom.

Put the tomato and bread slices on the grill, season with salt and pepper, and cook for about 1 minute on each side. Transfer the bread to plates and put the mushrooms, cheese sides up, on the bread. Spread each mushroom with 1 to 2 teaspoons of pesto and then top with the tomatoes and onions. Serve right away.

DOUBLE-SMOKED BISON BURGERS WITH CARAMELIZED ONIONS

I am a relatively new convert to smoked paprika, and I will never go back. I keep finding new ways to use it, such as in the aioli for these burgers made with lean ground bison. Building these burgers, with the cheese-topped meat and continuing with the caramelized onions and paprika-spiked aioli, is a lesson in curbing temptation. Try the aioli on other meat and chicken sandwiches, and if you can't find bison, use lean beef for the burgers.

Serves 4

CARAMELIZED ONIONS

3 tablespoons olive oil

1 large red onion, very thinly sliced

1 tablespoon balsamic vinegar

Kosher salt and freshly ground pepper

BISON BURGERS

1½ pounds ground bison meat

Kosher salt and freshly ground black pepper

2 tablespoons canola oil

1 cup shredded smoked Gouda (about 3 ounces)

4 hamburger buns

Smoked Paprika Aioli (recipe follows)

TO MAKE THE CARAMELIZED ONIONS: In a medium sauté pan, heat the olive oil over medium-low heat and when hot, cook the onions for about 20 minutes, stirring occasionally, until soft and caramelized. Add the vinegar and season to taste with salt and pepper.

TO MAKE THE BURGERS: Season the bison meat with salt and pepper and form four burgers. In a large sauté pan, heat the oil until almost smoking and cook the burgers for about 3 minutes on each side. Remove from pan when rare to medium rare. Cook longer if you prefer better-done meat. During the final minute of cooking, top the burgers with the shredded cheese so that it can melt.

Serve the burgers on the hamburger buns topped with aioli and Caramelized Onions.

SMOKED PAPRIKA AIOLI

Makes about ¹/₂ cup

¹/₂ cup mayonnaise

1 teaspoon minced garlic

¹/₂ teaspoon smoked paprika

¹/₂ teaspoon fresh lemon juice

Kosher salt and freshly
ground pepper

Whisk together the mayonnaise, garlic, paprika, and lemon juice. Season to taste with salt and pepper and a few more drops of lemon juice, if needed.

BARBECUED CHICKEN BURGERS WITH COLESLAW

While it's not difficult to shred cabbage and carrots, if you buy a pre-cut coleslaw mix these burgers are even easier. You could also opt to douse the burgers with barbecue sauce rather than making the barbecue mayo, but I think the mayonnaise is mellower and slightly more stylish. Ground chicken is wetter and stickier than ground beef or turkey, and so it's a good idea to dampen your hands before working with it.

Serves 4

COLESLAW

¼ cup mayonnaise

¼ cup buttermilk

1 teaspoon lemon juice

½ teaspoon kosher salt

¼ teaspoon celery seed

1 cup finely shredded Savoy cabbage

1 cup finely shredded red cabbage

1 cup peeled and grated carrots

2 scallions, trimmed and sliced

Freshly ground pepper

CHICKEN BURGERS

1 pound ground chicken breast meat

2 ounces Cheddar cheese, grated (about ⅔ cup)

¼ cup grated white onion

2 tablespoons prepared barbecue sauce

1 teaspoon smoked paprika

½ teaspoon garlic powder

½ teaspoon kosher salt, plus more for sprinkling

Freshly ground black pepper

4 hamburger buns

Barbeque Mayonnaise (recipe follows)

TO MAKE THE COLESLAW: Whisk together the mayonnaise, buttermilk, lemon juice, salt, and celery seed until smooth. Add the cabbages, carrots, and scallions and toss well. Season to taste with pepper.

TO MAKE THE BURGERS: Spray the grilling grate of a gas or charcoal grill with vegetable oil spray. Heat the grill so that the heating elements or coals are medium hot.

Mix the chicken with the cheese, onion, barbecue sauce, paprika, garlic powder, and salt. With dampened hands, form four patties (you need wet hands because ground chicken is very moist and sticky). Season the patties with salt and pepper.

Preheat the grill to medium hot. Grill the burgers for about 4 minutes on each side, or until cooked through. Set the burgers on the buns and top with the Barbecue Mayonnaise and coleslaw. Serve right away.

BARBECUE MAYONNAISE

Makes about ¹/₂ *cup*

¹/₄ cup prepared barbecue sauce

¹/₄ cup mayonnaise

Kosher salt and freshly ground black pepper

Whisk the barbecue sauce into the mayonnaise until smooth. Season to taste with salt and pepper.

CHAPTER 8

BREAKFAST FOR DINNER

WHEN I WAS GROWING UP, BREAKFAST FOR DINNER WAS A TREAT. My sister and I were as happy to dig into an omelet or a stack of pancakes when the sun set as we were when it rose. Looking back, I realize those meals probably had more to do with my mom's energy level or depleted refrigerator than a desire to please us, but we didn't mind at all!

I have carried the tradition into life with my own kids. There are days when I am not in the mood for traditional dinner fare and so fill the gap with frittatas, pancakes, and French toast. I have even included a favorite recipe for granola as part of the chapter because why not eat something good and good for you in the evening?

Greg and I prefer omelets or fritattas, rather than the pancakes the kids beg for. Add a green salad and the meal is complete. I doubt you'll serve breakfast for dinner when you have adult guests (your kids' friends won't complain if you do!) but you will get some great ideas on the following pages for what to offer weekend overnighters or your own family for a weekend morning meal.

I am most apt to serve breakfast for dinner on those hectic nights when sports schedules, after-school activities, and late meetings make planning a more typical meal tricky. Guess what? No one objects!

ASPARAGUS, LEEK, AND FETA FRITTATA

Frittatas can be eaten warm or at room temperature, which makes them just about perfect for a meal that might be served in waves, as one hungry child after another arrives home. They are easy to make your own by varying the ingredients, and I find them simpler than quiches (no crust required!). A nonstick pan guarantees a perfect turnout every time.

Serves 6 to 8

10 stalks asparagus, thick or woody ends removed

1 large leek, root end trimmed

2 tablespoons unsalted butter

1 teaspoon kosher salt, plus more for seasoning

Freshly ground pepper

10 large eggs

1 cup half-and-half

4 ounces feta cheese, broken into small pieces

Preheat the oven to 350°F.

Remove the top inch of the asparagus tips and split them lengthwise. Cut the remaining stalks crosswise into very thin slices.

Split the leek in half lengthwise and slice the white end and the light green part of the stalk into half-moon-shaped slices about $1/4$-inch thick. (You will have about $1 1/2$ cups.) Put the leek slices in a large bowl of water and swish them around to rinse well, changing the water until it runs clear. Lift from the water with your hands or a slotted spoon and set aside.

Melt the butter in a 10-inch, oven-safe, nonstick sauté pan over medium heat until it begins to bubble. Reduce the heat to medium-low and cook the asparagus and leeks for about 10 minutes, or until the vegetables begin to soften. Season with salt and pepper and spread the vegetables evenly in the pan. Whisk together the eggs, half-and-half, and 1 teaspoon of salt. Season lightly with pepper. Pour into the pan with the asparagus and leeks and sprinkle the feta over the top of the frittata. Cook over medium heat for about 1 minute before transferring the pan to the oven for 20 to 25 minutes, or until set in the center.

SOFT-POACHED EGGS WITH SWEET POTATO HASH

Hash, popular these days with even the most high-end chefs, has always been a constant in my kitchen. I like making it with sweet potatoes instead of the more expected white potatoes for their texture, rich flavor, and reassuring color. The chorizo and sage make earthy partners for the spuds.

Serves 4

2 large sweet potatoes

1/3 cup olive oil

1/2 white onion, finely diced (about 6 tablespoons)

1 small red bell pepper, finely diced

2 links chorizo sausage (about 3 ounces each), finely diced

2 tablespoons chopped fresh sage

Kosher salt and freshly ground black pepper

2 tablespoons apple cider or white vinegar

4 large eggs

Microwave the sweet potatoes, one at a time, on high power for 7 to 8 minutes, or until fork-tender. Let the potatoes cool completely and then peel and cut into small dice. (You can also cook the sweet potatoes 24 hours ahead of time.)

In a medium sauté pan, heat the oil over medium-high heat and when shimmering, reduce the heat to low and cook the onion and pepper for 6 to 8 minutes or until softened. Add the sweet potato, chorizo, and sage, increase the heat to medium, and cook, stirring, for 2 to 3 minutes or until hot and the sausage is lightly browned. Season lightly with salt and pepper.

Meanwhile, fill a shallow saucepan with water and bring to a simmer and add the vinegar. Crack the eggs in a small bowl one at a time and carefully slide each one into the simmering water. Poach the eggs for about 3 minutes, until the whites become opaque but the yolks are still soft. If you feel confident, crack all four into a bowl and slide them into the water at once.

While the eggs are cooking, divide the hash between 4 serving plates.

Lift the eggs from the water with a slotted spoon, let them drain, and set on top of the hash. Season with salt and pepper to taste.

GOAT CHEESE, PEAR, AND PROSCIUTTO STRATA

A strata as rich and full-flavored as this earns its stripes on the dinner table when paired with a crisp arugula or frisée salad and a glass of wine. I especially like it in the fall and winter when pears are in the markets. If you don't like goat cheese, substitute mozzarella; if you don't have prosciutto, use ham. This can be assembled early in the day and popped in the oven when you get home. Serve the leftovers the next morning for breakfast, and if you're looking for something to make for brunch, look no further.

Serves 8 to 10

1 pound sliced white bread (about 12 slices)

2 tablespoons unsalted butter

3 ripe pears, cored and cut into ½-inch dice

8 large eggs

4 cups whole or low-fat milk

1 tablespoon Dijon mustard

1 teaspoon chopped fresh thyme leaves

1 teaspoon kosher salt

Freshly ground black pepper

6 ounces prosciutto, sliced

6 ounces goat cheese, crumbled

Lightly spray a 13 x 9 x 2-inch baking dish with flavorless vegetable spray. Cut the bread into 1-inch cubes and spread nearly half over the bottom of the pan. Reserve the remaining bread cubes.

In a medium sauté pan, heat the butter over medium heat and when it melts and bubbles, add the pears and sauté for 5 to 6 minutes or until they soften and begin to caramelize. Remove from the heat and set aside.

In a mixing bowl, beat together the eggs, milk, mustard, thyme, and salt. Season with pepper.

Spread half of the prosciutto, half the cheese, and half the pears over the bread. Spread the remaining bread cubes over these ingredients and then top evenly with the remaining prosciutto, cheese, and pears.

Pour the egg mixture over the strata and press lightly on the bread to submerge it in the liquid so that it soaks evenly. Cover with plastic wrap and refrigerate for at least 6 hours and up to 12 hours or overnight.

Take the strata from the refrigerator 30 minutes before baking.

Preheat the oven to 350°F. Remove the plastic wrap and bake the strata for 45 to 50 minutes or until the center is set and no longer wobbly. Serve warm.

FLUFFY BUTTERMILK PANCAKES, A.K.A. PERFECT PANCAKES

I make pancakes at least once a week and because I can't help myself, I constantly try to reinvent them. If you ask me, these are about as good as they get, and the double whammy of buttermilk and sour cream make them especially light and slightly tangy. Plus, they are the perfect backdrop for the syrup and mixed berries my kids like—and with three kids, we usually have three different choices for sweetening up the pancakes.

Serves 4 to 6

1 cup all-purpose flour

1 tablespoon granulated sugar

1 teaspoon baking powder

½ teaspoon baking soda

Pinch of salt

1 cup buttermilk

½ cup sour cream

½ cup whole milk

2 tablespoons olive oil

1 large egg

Whisk together the flour, sugar, baking powder, baking soda, and salt.

In a separate bowl, whisk the buttermilk with the sour cream, milk, oil, and egg. Add the buttermilk mixture to the dry mixture and whisk lightly to combine.

Lightly spray a griddle or skillet with vegetable spray and heat over medium heat. When hot, ladle the batter onto the griddle and cook the pancakes until the edges begin to dull and small bubbles break on the surface and remain open. Flip and cook for about 30 seconds longer, or until lightly browned. Serve immediately.

Dressed-Up Pancake

When you make the batter, you can stir in blueberries, sliced strawberries, chopped bananas, or diced pears for extra-special pancakes (or to use up some fruit you have hanging around).

To please my kids or guests who might be sitting at the table, I sometimes enhance the flavor of maple syrup by heating it gently with a handful of fresh raspberries or blueberries.

Don't have maple or pancake syrup on hand? No worries. Here's a quick recipe for a quick stovetop syrup:

HOMEMADE SYRUP

Makes about 1 cup

1 cup packed brown sugar
(dark or light)

1 cup granulated sugar

1 cup water

Pinch of salt

Bring everything to a boil over medium-high heat. Reduce the heat and simmer for about 3 minutes, stirring occasionally, until the sugar dissolves. Voilà!

APPLE SOUFFLÉ PANCAKE

I've liked this puffy pancake since my grandmother made one pretty similar to mine, satisfying my appreciation for eggs and fruit together. And because I usually always have eggs and apples around, this easy-to-make dish is a familiar one at our dinner table—and shows up for other meals, as well.

Serves 4

3 large eggs

½ cup milk

2 tablespoons sugar

2 tablespoons all-purpose flour

Pinch of salt

2 tablespoons unsalted butter

2 apples, peeled and thinly sliced, such as Gala, Rome, or Honey Crisp

½ teaspoon ground cinnamon, optional

Maple syrup, for serving

Preheat the oven to 400°F.

Whisk the eggs with the milk and 1 tablespoon of the sugar. Whisk in the flour and salt until smooth.

Melt the butter in an oven-safe skillet over medium heat and when it begins to bubble, add the apples and cook for 2 to 3 minutes, tossing very gently. Sprinkle the remaining tablespoon of sugar and the cinnamon, if using, over the apples and cook for 2 to 3 minutes longer or until tender.

Pour the batter into the skillet and transfer it to the oven. Bake for 10 to 12 minutes or until the mixture sets and puffs slightly. Serve hot from the oven, sprinkled with more cinnamon, if desired, and with maple syrup.

My Apple Preferences

Some apples are crisp and juicy, others sweet and soft, and some tart and firm. Happily, they are easy to find, often from local growers. Here are my favorites for eating, baking, and cooking:

- **Eating apples** (crisp and juicy with tart flavor): Honeycrisp, Braeburn, Gala, and McIntosh
- **Baking apples** (these hold their shape in the oven): Baldwin, Cortland, Rome
- **Cooking apples** (I use these mainly for applesauce): Gala, Golden Delicious, and Granny Smith

LEMON-RICOTTA SILVER DOLLAR PANCAKES

While the buttermilk pancakes on page 190 are outstanding, I like a change now and again in the pancake department. Lightly kissed with lemon zest and lemon extract, these are seductively delicate and airy and a welcome change from the expected.

Serves 6; makes about 28 pancakes

1 cup all-purpose flour

¹/₃ cup granulated sugar

2 ¹/₂ teaspoons baking powder

¹/₄ teaspoon salt

1 cup ricotta cheese

1 ¹/₄ cups whole milk

1 ¹/₂ teaspoons grated lemon zest

³/₄ teaspoon lemon extract

2 large eggs, separated

Confectioners' sugar, for dusting

Whisk together the flour, sugar, baking powder, and salt.

In another bowl, whisk together the ricotta, milk, lemon zest, lemon extract, and egg yolks. Add the dry ingredients and mix well.

In a clean, dry bowl with an electric mixer, beat the egg whites until soft peaks form. Gently fold the beaten egg whites into the ricotta mixture and let the batter rest for 3 minutes.

Lightly spray a griddle or large skillet with vegetable spray and heat it over medium heat.

Drop large tablespoons of batter onto the griddle and cook for 2 to 3 minutes on each side. The pancakes will measure about 3 inches across. To prevent burning, don't let the griddle get too hot. The pancakes will look slightly dull and a few bubbles will form on the surface when they are ready to flip.

Serve dusted with confectioners' sugar or keep the pancakes warm in the oven.

APRICOT, HONEY, AND ALMOND GRANOLA

I am crazy about this crunchy granola—and I'm pretty proud about how it turned out. You might not think of eating cereal for dinner, but if your household is anything like mine, some nights that's all anyone can manage! And so, if you're going to depend on cereal, why not make sure it's the best one going. With milk and fresh fruit, this fits the bill. I took some of this granola to my trainer when I was developing recipes for the book and while I dutifully ran on the treadmill, she ate the entire bag! I was happy to see I am not the only one with zero willpower.

Makes about 6 cups

2 ½ cups old-fashioned rolled oats

1 cup diced dried apricots

½ cup sliced almonds

¼ cup sunflower seeds

¼ cup shredded sweetened coconut

¼ cup raisins

¼ cup honey

¼ cup unsalted butter

2 tablespoons packed brown sugar

Preheat the oven to 325°F. Lightly spray a large, rimmed baking sheet with cooking spray.

Toss together the oats, apricots, almonds, sunflower seeds, coconut, and raisins.

In a small pot, bring the honey, butter, and brown sugar to a boil. Stir to blend and then remove from the heat and spoon the honey mixture over the fruit and nuts. Mix lightly.

Spread the granola on the prepared baking sheet in an even layer. Bake for about 30 minutes, stirring once, until lightly golden brown.

Let the granola cool completely on the baking sheet before serving. Store the granola in an airtight container.

BLUEBERRY STREUSEL FRENCH TOAST

I like to set this up in the morning so it's ready to go when I get home from work. It's a handy recipe because it bakes in the oven and you don't have to tend the stove. It's a real winner, particularly when blueberries are in season.

Serves 8 〜〜〜〜〜〜〜〜〜〜〜〜〜〜〜〜〜〜〜〜〜〜〜

FRENCH TOAST

1 loaf challah or brioche (about 1 pound), cut into 3/4-inch-thick slices

6 large eggs

3 cups whole milk

1/3 cup sugar

1 1/2 teaspoons ground cinnamon

1 teaspoon vanilla extract

3 cups fresh blueberries

STREUSEL TOPPING

3/4 cup all-purpose flour

3/4 cup packed brown sugar

3/4 cup old-fashioned rolled oats

8 tablespoons (1 stick) cold unsalted butter, cut up into small pieces

Maple syrup, for serving

TO MAKE THE FRENCH TOAST: Lightly spray a 13 x 9 x 2-inch baking dish with vegetable spray. Cover the dish with a single layer of bread slices.

Whisk together the eggs, milk, sugar, cinnamon, and vanilla and pour enough of the mixture over the bread to cover it evenly (about half the mixture). Sprinkle half the blueberries over the bread.

Lay the rest of the bread slices in the dish and pour the remaining egg mixture over it. Lightly press on the bread slices to insure they are saturated with egg. Let the French toast soak for about 15 minutes or up to 8 hours, covered and refrigerated.

Preheat the oven to 350°F.

TO MAKE THE STREUSEL TOPPING: Put the flour, sugar, and oats in a food processor and pulse just to mix. Add the butter, piece by piece, pulsing until the mixture is crumbly.

Sprinkle the streusel topping evenly over the French toast. Scatter the remaining blueberries over the streusel.

Bake for 40 to 45 minutes or until set in the center and the top is golden brown. Serve with maple syrup.

The Right Bread for French Toast

French toast is an ideal way to use up slightly stale bread, those quarter or half loaves languishing in the bread box. While this is practical, when I have a choice, I always suggest using densely crumbed, egg-based brioche or challah. Both breads are gorgeously rich and perfectly textured for soaking up the sweet egg bath.

CINNAMON-WALNUT QUICK BREAD

Bet you can't eat just one slice! This is a favorite at Aux Délices, and once you sink your fork into the super-moist bread, you will understand why. It's addictive. I try not to make it too often at home because, frankly, I can't resist it. Pair it with soft scrambled eggs for a quick supper.

Makes one 9-inch loaf

2 cups all-purpose flour

1 teaspoon baking soda

1 teaspoon baking powder

½ cup (1 stick) unsalted butter, at room temperature

1 cup granulated sugar

2 large eggs

1 teaspoon pure vanilla extract

1 cup sour cream

FILLING

3 tablespoons finely chopped walnuts

2 tablespoons granulated sugar

1½ teaspoons ground cinnamon

Preheat the oven to 325°F.

Whisk together the flour, baking soda, and baking powder in a small bowl.

In the bowl of an electric mixer fitted with a paddle attachment, cream the butter and sugar on medium-high speed until well mixed. Add the eggs, one at a time, and beat until incorporated. Scrape down the sides of the bowl once or twice. Add the vanilla and then alternate adding the sour cream with the dry ingredients until mixed. Scrape the bottom of the bowl once or twice while mixing.

TO MAKE THE FILLING: Mix together the walnuts, sugar, and cinnamon.

Spoon half of the batter into a 3 x 9 x 5-inch loaf pan. Sprinkle half of the filling over the batter and then add the rest of the batter to the pan. Sprinkle the rest of the filling over the top of the loaf. Bake for 55 to 60 minutes or until a toothpick inserted in the center comes out dry.

DINNERTIME BURRITOS

When you bite into this burrito packed with scrambled eggs, cheese, and avocado you're getting a lot more than eggs for dinner. The substantial handheld meal can be customized to meet the tastes of your family or to use up leftovers, such as grilled or roasted veggies, brown rice, prosciutto, or chicken—even refried beans. If I have cilantro, I add that, and a heaping tablespoon of sour cream adds extra zip. When the burritos are chunky, the generous size of "burrito tortillas" makes them easier to roll and fold.

Serves 4

1 tablespoon unsalted butter

8 large eggs, lightly beaten

Kosher salt and freshly ground black pepper

4 burrito-sized or soft-taco-sized tortillas

1½ cups grated Cheddar or mozzarella cheese

8 slices ham, cut into thin slices

1 avocado, pitted and sliced

½ cup hot or mild store-bought salsa (use your favorite)

In a large sauté pan, heat the butter over medium heat. When melted, pour the beaten eggs into the pan and stir them with a fork for 3 to 4 minutes to softly scramble. Season with salt and pepper.

Heat the tortillas in a sauté pan over low heat or in the microwave.

Lay the tortillas flat on a work surface and divide the scrambled eggs among them. Top with equal amounts of cheese, ham, and avocado. Top with about 1 tablespoon of salsa and roll up the burrito. Tuck in the ends and serve, seam-side down.

If not serving right away, keep the burritos warm in a 200°F oven until ready to serve.

BLT BRUSCHETTA

Here all my breakfast favorites are piled on top of crusty sourdough toast: eggs, bacon, and tomatoes crowned with dressed arugula. Sophisticated enough for dinner and easy enough to make on the fly, you will want to make these open sandwiches often. Scramble or poach the eggs instead of frying them, and if you're not in the mood for eggs, substitute avocado. Outstanding!

Serves 4

¼ cup mayonnaise

1 teaspoon Dijon mustard

Kosher salt and freshly ground black pepper

8 slices bacon

4 Roma tomatoes, cored and cut into ¼-inch slices

4 slices sourdough bread, each about ½-inch thick

2 ounces baby arugula (about 4 handfuls)

2 tablespoons extra-virgin olive oil

4 large eggs

In a small dish, whisk together the mayonnaise and mustard and season to taste with salt and pepper. Set aside.

In a large sauté pan, cook the bacon over medium heat for 3 to 4 minutes on each side or until crispy. Drain on paper towels and cover loosely with aluminum foil to keep warm.

Drain the excess bacon fat and then put the tomato slices in the same pan. Season lightly with salt and pepper and cook for about 1 minute on each side or just until softened.

Toast the sourdough bread slices and spread each with about 1 tablespoon of the mayonnaise mixture. Top each with the bacon and tomato slices.

Meanwhile, toss the arugula with the olive oil and season to taste with salt and pepper.

Spray a nonstick frying pan with flavorless vegetable spray and heat the pan over medium heat. When hot, crack the eggs into the pan, season with salt and pepper, and cook for 3 to 4 minutes or until the whites are opaque and the yolks are warm but still runny.

Put a fried egg on top of each bruschetta. Top each egg with a small handful of arugula and serve immediately.

SIDE SHOWS

EVERYONE LIKES SIDE DISHES, BUT FEW OF US WANT TO FUSS OVER THEM. The sides should never be more complicated than the main course, right? In this chapter, I offer a number of ideas for fresh green veggies, and to meet everyone's requirements for carbs, I have suggestions for potatoes, couscous, and polenta. And speaking of carbs, both the corn cakes and cornbread in this chapter are perfect for sopping up any juices on the plate.

I grew up eating a combination of frozen, canned, and fresh vegetables and now as an adult I can't seem to get enough of the fresh sort. I like to eat veggies when they are at the height of their season for the best flavor and nutrition—and along the way, support local farmers. It's a good idea to roast or grill any vegetables that are languishing in the refrigerator. Once they are cooked, you'll be tempted to add them to sandwiches, omelets, and stir-frys.

Where I live in Connecticut, the corn season is short but glorious, and most people I know eat fresh corn as often as they can. Choose plump ears with fresh-looking green husks and brownish, bushy silk. Buy corn on the day it was picked and plan to eat it within hours, since the sugars convert to starch as soon as it's harvested. Tomatoes are best in the summer, too. Try various heirloom varieties if your farmers' market carries them: juicy and so, so delicious. For all spring and summer vegetables—asparagus, garden peas, zucchini, and beans—eat them fresh-picked and often. Tomatoes should not be refrigerated as the cool temps turn them mealy. In the fall and winter, I rely more often on squashes, potatoes, broccoli, and cabbages. Sweet and white potatoes, beets, and squashes, the so-called "storage" vegetables, will keep for up to a month in a cool, dry place. More perishable ones do well in the refrigerator for a day or two.

With just a little attention, side dishes take their rightful place on the dinner plate. Truth be told, I could happily eat two or three of these and skip the main course altogether for a totally satisfying vegetarian meal.

SWEET CORN SUCCOTASH

This is not your mother's succotash, made as it is with edamame, corn, and bell peppers. It's colorful, has a pleasing "bite," and tastes oh so good, especially as the bacon provides a hint of smokiness.

Serves 6

4 ears fresh corn, husked, with silks removed

2 tablespoons olive oil

2 slices bacon, thinly sliced

½ cup peeled and finely diced red onion

1 red bell pepper, seeded and finely diced

1 garlic clove, minced

8 ounces fresh or frozen, thawed, and shelled edamame

1 teaspoon chopped fresh thyme

Kosher salt and freshly ground black pepper

Hold the corn cobs upright on a work surface and, using a small knife, scrape the kernels from the cobs. Discard the cobs.

In a large sauté pan, heat the oil over medium heat until shimmering and cook the bacon for 2 to 3 minutes, or until golden brown and beginning to crisp.

Add the red onion, red pepper, and garlic and sauté for 4 to 5 minutes, or until the vegetables are tender. Stir in the corn, edamame, and thyme and cook for 2 to 3 minutes longer or until the vegetables are tender and the succotash is heated through. Season to taste with salt and pepper.

CARROTS WITH GINGER AND BLACK CURRANTS

I noticed this side dish on a menu for Trotters to Go, Chicago chef Charlie Trotter's outstanding take-out place. The combo of ingredients sounded intriguing and so I set about coming up with my own version. It's great! The sweet currants and somewhat spicy ginger are perfect accents for the carrots.

Serves 4 to 6

1 pound carrots, peeled and cut into ¼-inch-thick slices

1 tablespoon unsalted butter

2 teaspoons freshly grated fresh ginger

1 cup vegetable or chicken stock, preferably homemade

3 tablespoons dried black currants

Kosher salt and freshly ground black pepper

Put the carrots, butter, and ginger in a large sauté pan. Add the stock and bring to a boil over medium-high heat. Reduce the heat and simmer for 12 to 15 minutes or until the carrots are fork-tender and most of the liquid has evaporated. Toss in the currants and season to taste with salt and pepper.

PARMESAN AND BALSAMIC ROASTED CAULIFLOWER

Vegetables roasted with cheese are happily commonplace these days, and no one can deny their scrumptiousness. The trick is to be judicious with the cheese; you don't want to blanket the cauliflower with it and obscure the great flavor of the veg. I love the zing the white balsamic vinegar provides.

Serves 4

1 large head cauliflower, trimmed

3 tablespoons olive oil

3 tablespoons grated Parmesan cheese

¾ teaspoon kosher salt

Freshly ground black pepper

1 tablespoon, plus 2 teaspoons white balsamic vinegar

Preheat the oven to 400°F.

Cut the cauliflower into small florets. Put them in a bowl and toss with the oil, Parmesan, and salt. Season with pepper.

Spread the florets in a single layer on a nonstick baking sheet and roast for about 25 minutes or until golden brown and tender. Stir once during the roasting.

Transfer the roasted cauliflower to a bowl and toss gently with the vinegar. Taste and season with more salt and pepper, if needed. Serve right away.

STIR-FRIED GREEN BEANS

Green beans are pretty much a staple in our house, and perhaps in yours, too. Every now and then I change them up with Asian spices and the tang of chili paste. The splash of balsamic vinegar—decidedly not an Asian ingredient—provides just the right amount of sweetness.

Serves 4

2 tablespoons soy sauce

2 tablespoons chili-garlic paste or any Thai-style chili sauce

1 tablespoon balsamic vinegar

1 teaspoon granulated sugar

12 ounces green beans or haricots verts, trimmed

2 tablespoons sesame oil

3 scallions, trimmed and thinly sliced, white and light green parts

1 garlic clove, thinly sliced

1 tablespoon peeled and grated fresh ginger

Kosher salt and freshly ground black pepper

Whisk together the soy sauce, chili paste, vinegar, and sugar until the sugar dissolves.

Bring a pot of salted water to a boil and cook the beans for 3 to 4 minutes, or until bright green and beginning to soften. Drain the beans.

Meanwhile, in a medium sauté pan, heat the sesame oil over medium heat and sauté the scallions, garlic, and ginger for about 1 minute. Add the soy sauce mixture and heat for about 30 seconds, stirring, until bubbling and thick. Add the drained beans and toss them with the sauce until coated. Season to taste with salt and pepper and serve immediately.

Shock Therapy

If you want to blanch green vegetables—green beans, haricots verts, broccoli, Brussels sprouts, asparagus, and so on—ahead of time to eliminate an extra pot on the stove at dinner time, do what restaurant chefs do and shock them in ice water as soon as they are blanched. The frigid water immediately halts the cooking process so the vegetables are perfectly cooked and just a little crisp. It also preserves their bright green color.

To shock them, fill a bowl with cold water and ice cubes and plunge the blanched veggies—which, depending on the vegetable, will take various amounts of time, none very long, to blanch—in it as soon as you lift them from the boiling water. They only need about 30 seconds in the arctic bath so almost as soon as they are submerged you can lift them out. Let them dry spread out on paper towels. They are ready for stir-frying, sautéing, or any other use.

You can shock vegetables 20 or 30 minutes before you will need them, or do so earlier in the day and refrigerate them. If they are refrigerated, let them sit at room temp for 15 or 20 minutes before cooking further.

GRILLED ASPARAGUS WITH ORANGE GREMOLATA

I love to grill asparagus and once you try it, you'll love it, too. So easy, so quick. Dressing it with an orange-spiked gremolata is perfect, and the taste is a little mellower than the more traditional lemon. The gremolata would taste great with broccoli, too, dressing it up as it does the asparagus. If you prefer, you can steam or oven-roast the asparagus.

Serves 4

GREMOLATA

3 tablespoons finely chopped flat-leaf parsley

2 teaspoons grated orange zest

1 large garlic clove, minced

1 tablespoon extra-virgin olive oil

Kosher salt and freshly ground black pepper

ASPARAGUS

1 pound asparagus, woody ends removed

1 tablespoon olive oil

Kosher salt and freshly ground black pepper

TO MAKE THE GREMOLATA: Mix together the parsley, orange zest, and garlic. Add the oil and stir to mix. Season to taste with salt and pepper.

TO COOK THE ASPARAGUS: Spray the grilling grate of a gas or charcoal grill with vegetable oil spray. Preheat the grill to medium hot.

If the asparagus have thick, woody stems, snap them off. Peel the stems and lay the asparagus in a shallow dish. Sprinkle with oil and season with salt and pepper.

Lay the asparagus spears directly on the grilling grate (perpendicular to the grate so that they do not fall through). You could also grill the asparagus in a grilling basket. Grill the asparagus, turning a few times, for about 5 minutes, or until tender. Transfer to a serving plate, scatter the gremolata over the asparagus, and serve.

BROCCOLI WITH LEMON AND PINE NUTS

While I have nothing against steamed broccoli, which finds its way onto many dinner tables across the land, I like it much better roasted. It deepens the flavor of the broccoli, and when it's accented with this simple lemon vinaigrette, it climbs the ladder of vegetable side dishes. I am a big fan of lemon zest and so like to scatter it over the veg just before serving to pick up the flavors even more.

Serves 4

1 large head broccoli (1 to 1½ pounds), sliced lengthwise into long pieces

3 tablespoons olive oil

Kosher salt and freshly ground black pepper

2 tablespoons pine nuts

1 small shallot, minced

1 tablespoon lemon juice

2 tablespoons extra-virgin olive oil

Grated lemon zest (optional)

Preheat the oven to 350°F.

Spread the broccoli in a shallow roasting pan, toss it with the 3 tablespoons of olive oil, and season lightly with salt and pepper. Roast for about 40 minutes, tossing halfway through, until the broccoli is tender and golden brown.

Meanwhile, in a small, dry skillet, toast the pine nuts over medium-low heat for 2 to 3 minutes, or until they darken a shade or two and are fragrant. Shake the pan to prevent them from burning. Remove the pan from the heat and let the pine nuts cool.

Whisk together the shallot, lemon juice, and ½ teaspoon of salt, stirring until the salt dissolves in the lemon juice. Whisk in the 2 tablespoons of extra-virgin olive oil.

Transfer the broccoli to a serving platter and drizzle the lemon vinaigrette over it. Scatter the pine nuts over the broccoli. If desired, scatter some grated lemon zest over it, too. Serve right away.

GRILLED ZUCCHINI WITH CHILE AND MINT

If you like zucchini as much as I do, you will appreciate this side dish, perfect in high summer when every vegetable garden and farmers' market has a super abundance of the mild, green squash. I find the flavors of lemon, garlic, and mint great with zucchini. The amounts listed here could be a starting point for your taste, which might prefer a little more garlic, less mint, or whatever.

Serves 4

3 small zucchini (about 12 ounces)

3 tablespoons olive oil

Kosher salt and freshly ground black pepper

2 teaspoons fresh lemon juice

½ teaspoon dried red pepper flakes

1 garlic clove, minced

2 tablespoons chopped fresh mint leaves

Trim the ends of the zucchini and then cut the squash on the bias into ¼- to ½-inch-thick slices. The more angled the slant of the cut (and therefore the longer the slices), the easier the squash will be to grill. Drizzle with 1 tablespoon of the oil and season with salt and pepper.

Preheat a gas or charcoal grill to medium hot.

Spread the zucchini slices directly on the grill's grate and grill for about 2 minutes on each side or until lightly browned.

Transfer the zucchini slices to a plate or shallow bowl.

Mix together the remaining 2 tablespoons of olive oil with the lemon juice, red pepper flakes, and garlic. Drizzle the vinaigrette over the grilled zucchini, sprinkle with the mint, and season to taste with salt and pepper.

RICOTTA CORN CAKES

When it's summertime in the Northeast where I call home, sweet corn is one of the season's glories. I usually just eat it straight off the cob, but now and then I look for another way to serve it. These corn cakes offer a nice change: delicate and tasting just slightly of cheese. They are lovely alongside a roasted or grilled chicken breast or salmon steak.

Makes about 14 pancakes

2 ears fresh corn, husked, with silks removed

1 cup all-purpose flour

1 cup milk

1/2 cup ricotta

2 large eggs, beaten

Kosher salt and freshly ground black pepper

2 tablespoons chopped chives

Olive oil, as needed

Hold the corn cobs upright on a work surface, and using a small knife, scrape the kernels from the cobs. Discard the cobs.

Mix together the flour, milk, ricotta, and eggs and season with salt and pepper. Stir in the corn and chives.

Heat about 2 tablespoons of oil in a large skillet over medium heat. When the oil is hot, ladle about 1/4 cup of the batter into the pan and cook the corn cakes for about 2 minutes to a side. The cakes should be about 3 inches across. Lower the heat slightly if necessary for even cooking and add more oil to the skillet as needed.

Serve the corn cakes hot or warm.

POLENTA WITH SAGE AND BACON

Don't be put off by polenta. It may sound exotic and perhaps hard to cook but it's just not so. Polenta is nothing more mysterious than cornmeal with an Italian name that is cooked in water or stock until tender, smooth, and thickened. I love it with beef stew or any other braised dish because it's so good for soaking up juices left on the plate. It's also fantastic with grilled steak, salmon, and chicken. The bacon and sage in this recipe make the final dish especially rich and delicious.

Serves 6

4 slices bacon, cut into ½-inch slices

2 tablespoons chopped fresh sage leaves

2 cups chicken stock, preferably homemade

2 cups whole milk

1 cup polenta

¾ teaspoon kosher salt

1 tablespoon unsalted butter

Freshly ground black pepper

Cook the bacon in a medium-size saucepan over medium heat until crispy and the fat is rendered. Lift the bacon from the pan with a slotted spoon, leaving the fat behind. Drain the bacon on paper towels.

Discard all but 1 tablespoon of the bacon fat and cook the sage for about 30 seconds over medium heat. Add the stock and milk to the pan and bring to a boil. Slowly add the polenta to the boiling liquid, whisking to break up any clumps. Whisk in the salt, lower the heat to medium-low, and cook for 6 to 8 minutes, whisking continuously until smooth and creamy.

Add the butter and season to taste with pepper. Whisk until the butter is incorporated into the polenta and then stir in the bacon. Alternatively, serve the polenta with the bacon crumbled on top. Serve right away, while hot.

PESTO SMASHED POTATOES

Fresh pesto—bursting with herbaceous basil, salty Parmesan cheese, and fruity olive oil—blends gloriously with many foods, but in my book nothing beats pesto and olive oil–rich potatoes. Once you serve these pesto-laced mashers, they will be in demand for all eternity.

Serves 4

1 ½ pounds Yukon Gold or creamer potatoes, halved if large

⅓ cup extra-virgin olive oil

¼ cup Basil Pesto (page 151)

Kosher salt and freshly ground black pepper

Put the potatoes in a large saucepan or pot of salted water and bring to a boil. The potatoes should not crowd the pan. Reduce the heat and simmer briskly for about 15 minutes or until tender when pierced with a fork. Drain the potatoes and return them to the pot.

With a fork or potato masher, smash the potatoes until almost smooth with a few lumps remaining. Drizzle with the olive oil and stir in the pesto. Season to taste with salt and pepper and serve hot.

My Endless Love for Potatoes

Unadventurous diners are often described as "meat-and-potato" eaters, and while I understand the expression, I find both meat and potatoes fascinating ingredients. Potatoes are varied and versatile, and while most spuds can be used for any recipe calling for them, it's helpful to know their differences and best uses. Here's a look at how I think of them:

Baking potatoes: These starchy specimens have names like russet, Idaho, Maine, Russet Arcadia, Russet Burbar, Goldrush, and Long White. These names can be bandied about widely, so you might see a potato labeled as a Maine Russet or a Russet Burbank. When baked whole, these potatoes are light and fluffy, and their thick skins form a self-contained jacket. They are good for French fries and other fried preparations because of their high starch content. I use these for mashed potatoes, too.

Boiling potatoes: With smooth, thin skins, these are not recommended for baking whole, but instead are wonderful in soups, casseroles, and potato salads. They are my first choice for roasting and grilling because they hold their shape so well. While many cooks mash them, they tend to be a little lumpy rather than smooth and fluffy. Sometimes called all-purpose or waxy potatoes, boiling potatoes have names such as Round White, Red, Yellow, Red Bliss, Yellow Finnish, Yukon Gold, Red La Rouge and Salad potatoes. Regardless of their name, these are moist tubers high in sugar and low in starch.

New potatoes: A new potato is any immature, small potato, dug from the earth before it grows to its full size. Most new potatoes widely sold are red-skinned, although this does not mean that all small, red-skinned potatoes are new, or that all new potatoes must have red skin. Their tender age is what makes them "new."

Creamer potatoes: These can be confused with new potatoes because they are young boiling potatoes. The most popular potatoes in this category are Yukon Gold and Red. Their tender flesh is moist and waxy without being too starchy. I like to use creamers for boiling, roasting, and in soups and stews.

OVEN-BAKED FRIES WITH PARMESAN AND ROSEMARY

These are just right with any of the burgers in Chapter 7, or try them alongside grilled steak or chicken. Perfection! A nice change from traditional French fries or baked potatoes and so easy to make. Little effort, big wallop!

Serves 4

2 russet potatoes

1/3 cup grated Parmesan cheese

1 tablespoon chopped fresh rosemary

1 garlic clove, minced

1 teaspoon salt

1/4 cup olive oil

Freshly ground black pepper

Preheat the oven to 400°F. Lightly spray a baking sheet with vegetable oil spray.

Split the potatoes in half lengthwise and then cut each half into six evenly sized wedges. Toss the wedges with the cheese, rosemary, garlic, and salt. Drizzle with the olive oil, season with pepper, and toss to mix.

Spread the potatoes evenly on the baking sheet and bake for about 35 minutes, or until tender and golden brown, turning once during baking.

BUTTERNUT SQUASH AND FARRO RISOTTO

I had a butternut squash and farro risotto once at The Dressing Room, Michel Nischan's restaurant in Westport, Connecticut. Totally enchanted, I went home to re-create it and am pretty pleased with the outcome. The farro is so toothy and earthy and the squash so smooth and sweet that each bite becomes an indulgence in contrasts. This makes a wonderful vegetarian main course. You can make the butternut squash "stock" ahead of time and refrigerate it for up to 24 hours, which makes the risotto pretty easy.

Serves 6 as a side dish; serves 4 as a main dish

1 (20-ounce) package peeled and cut butternut squash (from 1 large squash)

2 cups chicken or vegetable stock, preferably homemade

3 tablespoons olive oil

½ onion, finely diced

2 garlic cloves, minced

4 ounces wild or domestic cultivated mushrooms, finely chopped

1 cup farro

1 cup frozen peas, thawed

⅓ cup grated Parmesan cheese

1 teaspoon kosher salt

Freshly ground black pepper

In a large pot, cover the butternut squash with the chicken stock and about 3 cups of water and bring to a boil over medium-high heat. Cook for about 15 minutes to soften the squash so that it's fork-tender. Working in batches, transfer the squash and the cooking liquid to a blender, purée until smooth, and pour into a large bowl.

In a heavy, medium pot, heat the olive oil until shimmering and cook the onion and garlic for about 5 minutes until the onion begins to soften. Add the mushrooms to the pot and cook for 1 to 2 minutes, stirring until they begin to soften. Add another tablespoon of olive oil if needed.

Add the farro to the pot and stir to coat it with oil. It will begin to smell a little nutty. Slowly stir the butternut squash purée into the farro, a cup at a time. Don't add the next cup until the first is absorbed by the farro. This process will take about 25 minutes and the farro will absorb 6 to 7 cups of the purée. The farro should be just al dente with a little bit of chewiness.

Just before serving, stir in the peas, cheese, and salt and season to taste with pepper.

Nutty, Chewy,
and Good for You, Too!

From the first time I cooked farro, I've been a huge fan. Not only is it more nutritious than other grains, it's a complex carbohydrate with twice the protein and fiber of wheat. Farro has been cultivated since Biblical times. This is in part because it grows well in poor soil and so was transported easily by wandering peoples. Modern-day wheat, so versatile and easy to grow on America's vast plains and Russia's great steppes, quickly outpaced farro in production and popularity so that nowadays, farro is considered an exotic grain.

It is quite different from its wheat cousin and resembles spelt in taste and texture so that it is sometimes said to be the same thing. It is not, and while in some cases one can be substituted for the other, it's a good idea to use the grain called for in a specific recipe. Farro tastes a little nutty, is a little chewy, and stands up to strong flavors.

GOLDEN
ALMOND COUSCOUS

Couscous cooks in a flash and is so mild that it blends with any number of other ingredients and flavors. This dish, enlivened with almonds, cinnamon, and sugar, is a wonderful side dish to serve with the Moroccan Lamb Stew on page 140, Spiced Apricot Chicken on page 91, or anything you fancy.

Serves 4

1 tablespoon olive oil

½ cup whole blanched almonds

1 tablespoon unsalted butter

2 teaspoons sugar

¼ teaspoon cinnamon

1 cup couscous

Kosher salt and freshly ground black pepper

1 cup chicken stock

In a small sauté pan, heat the oil over medium-high heat and when hot, cook the almonds, stirring, for 1 ½ to 2 minutes, or until golden. Using a slotted spoon, transfer the almonds to paper towels to drain and cool.

Put the cooled almonds in the bowl of a food processor fitted with the metal blade. Add the butter, sugar, and cinnamon and pulse until the nuts are coarsely chopped.

In a medium-size, heatproof serving bowl or casserole dish with a tight-fitting lid, mix together the couscous and salt. Bring the chicken stock to a boil over high heat and then pour over the couscous. Cover tightly and set aside for 4 to 5 minutes.

Uncover the dish, fluff the couscous with a fork and then stir in the almonds. Season to taste with salt and pepper and serve.

SOUR CREAM CORNBREAD

The number of people who will be fed by this pan of crumbly-tangy cornbread depends on the size of the pieces and the size of the appetites. Any leftovers freeze beautifully, which I love, but of course in your family—as in mine—leftovers might be rare.

Serves 10 to 12

2 ¼ cups cornmeal

1 ¾ cups all-purpose flour

⅓ cup granulated sugar

4 teaspoons baking powder

1 ¼ teaspoons kosher salt

1 cup (2 sticks) unsalted butter, melted

1 cup sour cream

1 cup milk

2 large eggs

Preheat the oven to 350°F. Lightly spray a 13 x 9 x 2-inch baking pan with vegetable oil spray.

Whisk together the cornmeal, flour, sugar, baking powder, and salt. Set aside.

In another bowl, whisk the butter with the sour cream, milk, and eggs. Pour the wet ingredients into the dry ingredients and stir just until blended.

Scrape the batter into the prepared pan and bake for 30 to 35 minutes, until light golden brown and a toothpick inserted in the center comes out dry.

Let the cornbread cool a little before cutting into squares and serve warm or at room temperature.

SOMETHING SWEET

LIKE MOST PEOPLE, I LIKE A LITTLE SOME-THING SWEET AFTER DINNER. Just a few bites hit the spot, and so I don't save dessert for weekends or special occasions. I might not be setting a good example for my kids, but honestly, I don't think a little hurts. Because of this, I have packed this chapter with easy-to-make recipes for brownies, bars, cookies, and pies. When you take the 20 minutes needed to make semifreddo, your family will be impressed—and you'll be impressed because you don't need an ice cream machine. The fruit desserts are great, especially when the fruit is in season. I love the Nectarine and Blackberry Crisp in the summertime after an outdoor meal, and my kids like it topped with scoops of vanilla ice cream. After a hearty winter meal, the Tangelos with Lemon and Ginger are perfect. Any time of year, a cookie or brownie ends a meal on a happy note.

Because desserts are never absolutely "necessary," I like to keep them a little childlike—but not childish. My chocolate chip cookies have a touch of mint, the chocolate pudding is laced with mini marshmallows, and the ice cream sandwiches are almost over the top, but not quite. The Chocolate Espresso Bars are sophisti-cated, and the ginger cake is distinctly homespun, and yet both appeal to adults and kids alike.

At Aux Délices, we have a fantastic pastry department, headed by a chef who trained with the great Francois Payard, and so the sky is the limit when we plan the confections for the stores. At home, I am a little more moderate but no less en-chanted by the idea of dessert. I have found that whether you are cooking dinner for your family or entertaining friends at a party, a dessert ends the meal with style and smiles. It doesn't have to be fancy, but it does have to be good!

APPLE BARS

My dad's wife gave me this recipe for what she calls Apple Brownies. They bake up fairly thin and there's no chocolate in sight, so I changed the name simply to Apple Bars. Whatever you call them, they are scrumptious.

Makes 12 to 16 bars

CRUST

2 cups all-purpose flour

1/2 cup granulated sugar

1/2 teaspoon baking powder

1/2 teaspoon kosher salt

1 cup unsalted butter, slightly softened, cut into pieces

2 large egg yolks, beaten

APPLE FILLING

4 large, tart apples, preferably Rome, peeled and sliced into 1/4-inch-thick slices

3/4 cup granulated sugar

1/4 cup all-purpose flour

2 teaspoons ground cinnamon

Juice from 1/2 lemon

1 large egg white, lightly beaten

Preheat the oven to 350°F.

TO MAKE THE CRUST: Whisk together the flour, sugar, baking powder, and salt. Cut in the butter using a pastry cutter, or your fingers, work the butter into the flour until it becomes a coarse meal. Stir in the egg yolks until the dough becomes smooth.

Divide the dough in half and press half into the bottom of a 13 x 9 x 2-inch pan to form a thin bottom crust. (There will not be enough dough for anything but a thin crust.)

TO MAKE THE FILLING: Toss the sliced apples with the sugar, flour, cinnamon, and lemon juice. Spread the apple slices evenly over the crust.

Break off small pieces of the remaining dough and flatten them with your fingers by pressing them into the palm of one hand. They will be about the size of fifty-cent pieces or just smaller than the palm of your hand, but do not have to be uniform. As you make these discs, lay them over the apples to make an uneven top crust. Brush the top crust with the beaten egg white.

Bake for about 45 minutes until the top crust is light golden brown and the apples are bubbling slightly. Cool the bar cookies in the pan and then cut them into bars.

CHOCOLATE MARSHMALLOW PUDDING

Who doesn't like chocolate pudding? A few years ago, every high-end restaurant in the country put it on the menu, along with chocolate chip cookies, rice pudding, and banana splits, to appeal to the kid in all of us. It's been a menu item in our house forever, and this one, sweetened with tiny marshmallows, is irresistible.

Serves 6

¹⁄₃ cup granulated sugar

¹⁄₄ cup cornstarch

Pinch of kosher salt

3 cups whole milk

6 ounces good-quality semisweet chocolate, coarsely chopped

¹⁄₂ teaspoon pure vanilla extract

1¹⁄₂ cups mini marshmallows

Put the sugar, cornstarch, and salt in a heavy saucepan set over medium-low heat. Whisk in the milk and when the mixture comes to a low boil, simmer for 6 to 8 minutes, stirring constantly. When the mixture begins to thicken, add the chocolate and vanilla and whisk until the pudding is smooth and thick. Cook for 2 to 3 minutes longer over low heat.

Remove the pan from the heat. Gently fold in the marshmallows and stir for a minute or so or until they begin to melt.

Pour into a serving bowl or six individual pudding cups or dishes. Let the pudding cool slightly and then cover with plastic wrap so that the plastic sits directly on the pudding. Cool for 2 to 3 hours at room temperature until set, or refrigerate until chilled and set.

CHOCOLATE-CHUNK ICE CREAM SANDWICHES

This is one of those recipes that can be adjusted to your liking. You can eat the cookies without the ice cream . . . or scoop smaller amounts of cookie dough for smaller cookies . . . or scoop more dough onto the baking sheets for large sandwiches. Use a melon scoop or small ice cream scoop to make perfect-looking cookies . . . or not. But remember, the cookies are all about the chocolate, so use a high-quality brand.

Makes ten 3 1/2 -inch sandwiches

10 ounces good-quality bittersweet chocolate, finely chopped

1/2 cup, plus 1 tablespoon all-purpose flour

3 tablespoons unsweetened cocoa powder

1/4 teaspoon kosher salt

6 tablespoons unsalted butter, softened

1 cup granulated sugar

3 large eggs, at room temperature

1 teaspoon pure vanilla extract

1 cup good-quality semi-sweet chocolate chips

1 pint vanilla ice cream, slightly softened

Preheat the oven to 350°F. Lightly spray two baking sheets with vegetable spray.

Put the chopped chocolate in the top of a double boiler or a heatproof bowl set over barely simmering water on low heat. Stir the chocolate occasionally for about 5 minutes or until it melts. Remove the pan from the heat and cool for about 5 minutes. Alternatively, put the chocolate in a microwave-safe bowl or large glass measuring cup and microwave on medium power for 2 minutes. Remove and stir the chocolate. Microwave at 30 second intervals, stirring between each, until the chocolate blends into a liquid pool. It will not melt completely in the microwave and needs to be stirred.

Sift the flour, cocoa, and salt together into a bowl.

In the bowl of an electric mixer fitted with a paddle attachment and set on medium-high speed, beat the butter and sugar until the mixture resembles coarse meal. Add the eggs one at a time, beating well after each addition. Beat for another 3 to 4 minutes or until the dough is well mixed.

Add the cooled, melted chocolate and vanilla and beat well. Scrape the bottom of the bowl once or twice.

Lower the mixer speed to low and gradually add the flour mixture. Remove the bowl from the mixer and stir in the chocolate chips. Allow the batter to sit for about 5 minutes.

Scoop a well-rounded tablespoon of dough for each cookie onto the baking sheets, 2 to 3 inches apart. Dip the spoon in hot water in between scoops so that the dough releases easily. Using a wet fork, press each cookie to flatten it slightly.

Bake for about 15 minutes or until the cookies are dull on top and still a little soft. The cookies should be about $3\frac{1}{2}$ inches in diameter. Let them cool for 3 to 4 minutes on the baking sheets before transferring them to wire cooling racks. Let them cool completely.

Put a large spoonful of slightly softened ice cream on the flat side of ten of the cookies. Sandwich with ten more cookies and press gently. Wrap with plastic wrap and freeze for at least 2 hours and up to 3 days until firm.

COCONUT AND LIME CREAM PIE

I love the zip the lime gives this classic pie. We make a lot of these pies for Aux Délices, where they are insanely popular. Like coconut and lime? You're in luck!

Makes one 9-inch pie ⊃⊂⊃⊂⊃⊂⊃⊂⊃⊂⊃⊂⊃⊂⊃⊂⊃⊂⊃⊂⊃⊂⊃⊂⊃⊂

2 cups whole milk

1 cup coconut milk (not light)

²/₃ cup granulated sugar, divided

¼ teaspoon kosher salt

4 large egg yolks, beaten

¼ cup, plus 2 tablespoons all-purpose flour

2 tablespoons unsalted butter

1 teaspoon pure vanilla extract

Grated zest and juice of ½ lime

1 cup sweetened shredded coconut

1 baked 9-inch Deb's Flaky Pie Crust (page 236), or your favorite store-bought crust

Whipped cream, for garnish

In a saucepan, mix together the milk, coconut milk, ¹/₃ cup of the sugar, and salt, and bring to a boil over medium-high heat, stirring to mix well.

Meanwhile, in a bowl, whisk the egg yolks with the remaining ¹/₃ cup of sugar until pale yellow and blended. Whisk in the flour. Slowly stir half of the boiling liquid into the egg mixture to temper the eggs, whisking continuously. Return the custard to the pan and bring back to a gentle simmer. Let the custard boil for about 2 minutes, stirring constantly, or until slightly thickened.

Take the pan from the heat and add the butter, lime zest, and juice, and stir until smooth.

Add the coconut, stir to combine, and then pour into the baked pie shell.

Cover with plastic wrap and refrigerate for at least 6 hours or until set. Serve garnished with whipped cream.

DEB'S FLAKY PIE CRUST

Don't be afraid to make your own pie dough; it's not hard. This is a foolproof recipe that results in a buttery, flaky dough, but of course, if you would rather buy premade pie crust in the supermarket, go for it. Homemade tastes better, though!

Makes one 9-inch pie crust

³/₄ cup all-purpose flour

¹/₄ cup cake flour

1 teaspoon baking powder

¹/₂ teaspoon kosher salt

6 tablespoons cold butter

3 tablespoons ice-cold water

1 teaspoon white wine vinegar

Put the all-purpose flour, cake flour, baking powder, and salt in the bowl of an electric mixer fitted with a paddle attachment. With the mixer on low speed, add the butter, a tablespoon at a time, until the mixture resembles coarse meal. This will take 3 to 4 minutes.

Add the water and vinegar and mix for about 30 seconds longer, or until the dough begins to form a ball. Remove the dough from the mixer, shape it into a disk and wrap it in plastic wrap. Refrigerate for at least 1 hour.

Preheat the oven to 400°F.

On a lightly floured board, roll the chilled dough into a circle with a diameter of 11 to 12 inches. Gently press the dough into a 9-inch pie pan with the sides overhanging the rim. Trim the edges so that the dough is even with the edges of the pan. Lightly spray a piece of foil with vegetable oil spray and lay in on the crust, sprayed side down. Put pie weights or dried beans on top of the foil. This keeps the crust from puffing up during baking.

Bake for 8 to 9 minutes, or until the edges begin to turn golden brown. Remove from the oven and gently lift the foil from the pie pan. Use a fork to prick the bottom and sides of the crust in several places. Return it to the oven for 9 to 10 minutes longer or until light golden brown.

Let the pie crust cool completely set on a wire rack.

TANGELOS WITH LEMON AND GINGER

Who wants dessert after a big meal? Well. Okay. Maybe nearly everyone does . . . but there are times when a little fresh fruit hits the spot better than a big bowl of ice cream. I came up with this honeyed fruit dessert as a compromise between a sweet, sticky, rich dessert and a clementine. The ginger, honey, and spices are just right with the oranges, and because you have to make this ahead of time to give it time to chill, it's the ideal dessert for the busy cook.

Serves 6 to 8

³/₄ cup granulated sugar

¹/₃ cup peeled and finely chopped ginger

2 tablespoons honey

6 cardamom pods

3 star anise

1 cinnamon stick

Juice and grated zest of ¹/₂ lemon

1 tablespoon chopped fresh mint

6 tangelos, or navel or Cara Cara oranges

Fresh mint, for garnish

In a small saucepan, combine 1¹/₂ cups of water, the sugar, ginger, honey, cardamom pods, star anise, cinnamon stick, and lemon juice and zest. Bring to a boil over high heat, reduce the heat to low, and simmer for about 10 minutes. Add the chopped mint and remove from the heat.

Let the sauce cool to room temperature, cover, and refrigerate for at least 6 hours and up to 2 days.

Four to 6 hours before serving, slice the ends off the tangelos and peel them, removing all the white pith. Cut the tangelos crosswise into ¹/₂-inch-thick slices and arrange them on a shallow platter.

Drizzle the chilled syrup over the fruit and keep chilled. Garnish the plate with mint sprigs and serve.

LEMON BARS

As a self-described citrus freak, lemon bars seem to be appropriate all the time to me: after a meal, as a quick snack, with coffee, with tea, with a midnight TV show. The buttery crust is to die for!

Makes 12 to 14 bars ⧖⧖⧖⧖⧖⧖⧖⧖⧖⧖⧖⧖⧖⧖⧖⧖⧖

DOUGH

1 ³/₄ cups all-purpose flour

¹/₂ cup confectioners' sugar

¹/₄ cup cornstarch

Pinch of kosher salt

³/₄ cup (1 ¹/₂ sticks) cold unsalted butter, cut into small pieces

1 large egg, lightly beaten

FILLING

4 large eggs

1 cup granulated sugar

²/₃ cup fresh lemon juice

¹/₃ cup heavy cream

¹/₄ cup all-purpose flour

Pinch of kosher salt

TO MAKE THE CRUST: In the bowl of an electric mixer fitted with the paddle attachment, mix together the flour, confectioners' sugar, cornstarch, and salt on medium-low speed. With the mixer still running on medium-low speed, add the butter a few pieces at a time until the dough has a cornmeal-like consistency. Add the egg and mix for about 30 seconds or until the mixture forms a smooth dough.

Press the dough into a 13 x 9 x 2-inch pan so that it goes up the sides about 1 inch. Chill for 15 to 20 minutes.

Preheat the oven to 325°F. Line the dough with aluminum foil and weight the foil with pie weights or dry beans.

Bake for 20 to 25 minutes or until light golden brown. Remove the foil and let the crust cool for about 15 minutes.

TO MAKE THE FILLING: Whisk together the eggs, sugar, lemon juice, cream, flour, and pinch of salt until smooth. Pour into the cooled crust and bake for about 25 minutes or until set.

Let the bars cool in the pan until just warm. Refrigerate for at least 1 hour or until completely chilled. The bars can be refrigerated for up to 8 hours or overnight (if you refrigerate overnight, cover with plastic wrap). Cut into bars and serve.

NECTARINE AND BLACKBERRY CRISP

Fruit crisps are my go-to dessert in the summertime when local fruits and berries are at their luscious, juicy best. Quick and easy, they can be made ahead of time, and there's hardly a soul who doesn't smile when you bring one to the table. This one, with its oatmeal topping, is especially effortless. What's more, crisps are perfect paired with whipped cream or ice cream. Homemade ice cream is not necessary, but it would be divine!

Serves 8

FRUIT FILLING

8 ripe nectarines (about 2 1/2 pounds), pitted and cut into 1/2-inch-thick wedges

1 1/2 cups blackberries (12 ounces)

Grated zest and juice of 1 lemon

1/2 cup granulated sugar

1 tablespoon cornstarch

OATMEAL CRISP TOPPING

3/4 cup brown sugar

3/4 cup all-purpose flour

3/4 cup old-fashioned rolled oats

1/2 teaspoon ground cinnamon

1/2 cup (1 stick) cold unsalted butter, cut into small pieces

TO MAKE THE FRUIT FILLING: Preheat the oven to 375°F. Put an oven rack in the bottom third of the oven.

Mix together the nectarines, blackberries, and lemon juice and zest. In another bowl, mix the sugar with the cornstarch and then sprinkle this over the fruit. Toss gently to combine. Transfer the fruit to a 2 1/2-quart baking dish.

TO MAKE THE OATMEAL TOPPING: In the bowl of a food processor, mix together the brown sugar, flour, rolled oats, and cinnamon. Pulse to mix.

Add the butter, a few pieces at a time, pulsing after each addition. The topping should come together like wet sand.

Sprinkle the topping evenly over the fruit. Bake for about 45 minutes or until the fruit is bubbling hot and the topping is golden brown.

Serve the crisp hot or at room temperature.

CHOCOLATE ESPRESSO BARS

It's hard to argue with the flavor combination of chocolate and coffee, particularly when the two come together in these moist, fudgy bars. Take care not to overbake them or they won't have the right texture. Use your favorite bittersweet or semisweet chocolate for the recipe, the best you can afford and which you would happily eat plain, straight from the wrapper. That's my best advice when it comes to choosing chocolate for baking.

Makes 16 bars

8 ounces good-quality bittersweet chocolate

1 cup (2 sticks) unsalted butter

3 tablespoons instant espresso powder or granules

4 large eggs, at room temperature

2 cups granulated sugar

1 cup all-purpose flour

¼ cup unsweetened cocoa

Preheat the oven to 350°F. Lightly spray a 13 x 9 x 2-inch baking pan with vegetable oil spray.

In the top of a double boiler set over simmering water, melt together the chocolate and butter, stirring until smooth.

Meanwhile, dissolve the espresso in 3 tablespoons of boiling water. When the butter and chocolate melt, mix in the espresso and remove from the heat.

In the bowl of an electric mixer fitted with the paddle attachment and on medium-high speed, beat together the eggs and sugar for about 8 minutes until pale and creamy and the mixture forms a ribbon when the paddle is lifted. Remove the bowl from the mixer.

Whisk together the flour and cocoa and add to the batter. Whisk until incorporated. Add the chocolate mixture and whisk until combined. Transfer to the baking pan, smooth the surface, and bake for 25 to 28 minutes or until the edges just begin to set. The bars will seem underdone but don't let them overbake.

Let the bars cool in the pan, set on a wire rack, and when cool, cut into squares and serve.

Chocolate, Chocolate, Chocolate, and More Chocolate

I love good chocolate. While the popular supermarket brands work fine in most recipes, once you try quality chocolate and discover the differences in taste, you, too, will look for bars of Guittard and Ghirardelli (my favorites) for your chocolate desserts. These are bars of bittersweet chocolate you could happily eat just by unwrapping them, and when you chop, grate, melt, and otherwise include the ambrosial ingredient in baked goods or other desserts, the final result is heavenly.

Buying chocolate can be confusing these days, because connoisseurs often go on and on about chocolate liquor percentages. Oh, they might say, I tried a 70 percent chocolate the other day. Outstanding! You may not have a clue what they mean.

The percentages listed on some high-end chocolate bars refer simply to the amount of pure chocolate—chocolate liquor—in the final product. Unsweetened chocolate is 100 percent chocolate liquor, but when it comes to bittersweet and semisweet chocolates, the chocolate liquor is mixed with cocoa butter and sugar to make the final product, and so the percentage of chocolate liquor goes down. By definition, bittersweet and semisweet chocolate must be 35 percent chocolate liquor, which tells you something about a bar that has 60, 70, or higher percentages of chocolate liquor. The higher the content, the less sugar and therefore the more bitter the bar. Many chocolate lovers prefer their chocolate super bitter. My preferences fall between 64 and 72 percent.

I suggest you try a number of chocolate bars to find those that please you the most. It's not a difficult assignment. The only caveat is that if a recipe calls for bittersweet, semisweet, or dark chocolate, use them—do not try to substitute milk chocolate or unsweetened baking chocolate; neither will work. (In case the term "dark chocolate" confuses you, it simply refers to any sweetened chocolate without milk solids. In other words: semisweet or bittersweet.) The same advice goes the other way. A recipe that calls for unsweetened baking chocolate will not be successful if you substitute dark or milk chocolate. Regardless of the chocolate you decide to use, take care when handling it. If a recipe calls for melting the chocolate without the addition of an ingredient such as butter or cream, take great care. Recipes may instruct you to melt chopped chocolate over gently simmering water. Use a double boiler or a smaller pot set over a larger one to mimic a double boiler and keep the heat low. If even a droplet of moisture (steam) lands in the chocolate as it melts, it could

seize or stiffen. Once this happens, the chocolate can't be salvaged and must be tossed. You will have to start over again with more chocolate.

I am accustomed to taking great care, but you might prefer to melt chocolate in the microwave, which eliminates the moisture problem. Don't expect the chocolate to melt into a liquid pool in the microwave, but it will soften and look wet and shiny, at which time you can stir it so it liquefies. This might take a few tries: be careful not to let the chocolate burn. It can happen very quickly.

MINT CHOCOLATE CHIP COOKIES

My very favorite flavor of ice cream is mint chocolate chip, so I decided I needed a cookie to match. Luckily, Cyril Chaminade, the pastry chef at Aux Délices obliged my craving and we came up with this stunner. Our customers can't get enough of these and you'll see why the first time you make them. If you can find organic food coloring, use it.

Makes 2 dozen cookies

1 cup all-purpose flour

½ teaspoon baking soda

½ teaspoon kosher salt

½ cup (1 stick) unsalted butter, softened

⅓ cup, plus 1 tablespoon granulated sugar

⅓ cup packed light brown sugar

1 large egg

2 teaspoons peppermint extract

3 drops green food coloring

¾ cup semisweet chocolate chips

Whisk together the flour, baking soda, and salt.

In the bowl of an electric mixer fitted with the paddle attachment, cream the butter and both sugars on medium-high speed for 2 to 3 minutes or until light and fluffy. Add the egg and mix on medium speed, scraping the bowl once or twice. Mix in the dry ingredients and when incorporated, add the peppermint extract and food coloring, and mix until the color is even.

Stir in the chocolate chips, cover the bowl, and refrigerate for at least 2 hours.

Preheat the oven to 325°F. Lightly spray a baking sheet with vegetable oil spray.

Scoop the dough by rounded teaspoons onto the baking sheets, leaving about 1 inch between the cookies. Bake for 12 to 14 minutes, or until golden brown around the edges.

Let the cookies cool on the baking sheet for a few minutes before transferring to wire racks to cool completely and serve.

FRESH GINGER CAKE

This ordinary-looking cake is deceptive, packed as it is with powerful flavors, particularly the punch of fresh ginger. I bake it all year long, although I particularly like it in the fall when it fills the kitchen with warm, sensual aromas that say "autumn." And in case you're wondering about the difference between this and more typical gingerbread, this cake incorporates fresh ginger.

Serves 10

6 ounces fresh ginger, peeled

1 cup granulated sugar

1 cup dark black-strap molasses

1 cup canola oil

2 teaspoons baking soda

2 1/2 cups all-purpose flour

1/2 teaspoon ground cinnamon

1/2 teaspoon ground cloves

2 large eggs, lightly beaten

About 1/2 teaspoon fresh lemon juice

1/4 cup confectioners' sugar

Preheat the oven to 325°F. Grease a 9-inch round pan that is 3 inches deep and line it with a parchment paper circle cut to fit.

Cut the ginger into medium-size pieces and put in the bowl of a food processor. Add the granulated sugar and pulse until very smooth, like a paste. Mix in the molasses and canola oil.

In a saucepan, bring 1 cup of water to a boil over medium-high heat, add the baking soda, and when dissolved, stir in the molasses mixture.

Whisk together the flour, cinnamon, and cloves and then whisk into the molasses mixture until combined. Add the eggs and mix well.

Pour the batter into the prepared pan and bake for 60 to 65 minutes, or until a toothpick inserted in the middle of the cake comes out dry.

Meanwhile, in a small bowl, drizzle the lemon juice, a few drops at a time, over the confectioners' sugar, whisking until the glaze is thick and smooth. Set the glaze aside until needed.

Allow the cake to cool in the pan for 10 to 15 minutes and then turn out of the pan to cool completely on a wire rack. When cool, drizzle the glaze over the top of the cake and serve.

STRAWBERRY SEMIFREDDO

I can't think of an easier way to make a frozen dessert that is ice cream–like, without the bother of digging out the ice cream machine. You can substitute other fruits for the strawberries; peaches and raspberries come to mind. Once I make this, I can't keep it in the house. My kids are crazy for it.

Serves 8

1 pint strawberries, hulled

2 large egg yolks

3 large eggs

1 cup granulated sugar

½ teaspoon pure vanilla extract

1 ¾ cups heavy cream

Put a 10 x 5-inch stainless steel container in the freezer to chill.

In the bowl of food processor, process the strawberries until smooth. You will have about 2 cups.

Whisk together the egg yolks, eggs, sugar, and vanilla in the top of a double boiler or heatproof bowl. Set over a saucepan of simmering water and whisk for 6 to 8 minutes or until the mixture thickens and turns pale. Remove from the heat and let the mixture cool for a few minutes.

In the bowl of an electric mixer fitted with the whisk attachment, whip the cream until soft peaks form.

Gently stir the berry purée into the slightly cooled egg mixture until well mixed. Fold in the whipped cream just to combine.

Pour into the chilled container and freeze for at least 6 hours or overnight. Serve directly from the freezer.

INDEX